# A Modern Girl's Guide to the Perfect Single Life

Sarah Ivens is the Editor-in-Chief of *OK!* magazine in America. She has written for *Tatler*, *GQ*, *Cosmopolitan*, *Marie Claire*, *Men's Health*, *InStyle*, the *Daily Mail* and the *Observer*. She is a born and bred Londoner who now lives in Brooklyn, New York.

Sarah's first six books, *A Modern Girl's Guide to Getting Hitched*, *A Modern Girl's Guide to Networking*, *A Modern Girl's Guide to Dynamic Dating*, *A Modern Girl's Guide to Etiquette*, *A Modern Girl's Guide to Getting Organised* and *The Bride's Guide to Unique Weddings* are also published by Piatkus.

# A Modern Girl's Guide to the Perfect Single Life

*How to be single – and love it!*

## SARAH IVENS

PIATKUS

PIATKUS

First published in Great Britain in 2008 by Piatkus Books

Copyright © 2008 by Sarah Ivens

Reprinted 2008

A CIP catalogue record for this book
is available from the British Library

ISBN 978-0-7499-2870-4

Typeset in Sabon and Scala by Paul Saunders
Printed and bound in Great Britain by
Clays Ltd, St Ives plc

Papers used by Piatkus Books are natural, renewable and recyclable
products made from wood grown in sustainable forests and certified
in accordance with the rules of the Forest Stewardship Council.

**Mixed Sources**
Product group from well-managed
forests and other controlled sources
www.fsc.org  Cert no. SGS-COC-004081
© 1996 Forest Stewardship Council

FSC

Piatkus Books
An imprint of
Little, Brown Book Group
100 Victoria Embankment
London EC4Y 0DY

An Hachette Livre UK Company
www.hachettelivre.co.uk

www.piatkus.co.uk

# Contents

# Acknowledgements

Thanks to my lovely editors Sarah Rustin, Denise Dwyer and Alice Davis for their continued support and enthusiasm, and all the team at Piatkus and Little, Brown. Megan Hess, you've done it again – your illustrations are adorable. To all my lovely girlfriends who have let me investigate their sordid single lives and reprint the juiciest bits of it, I love you – you're brave. And to the boys in my life: thanks for your honesty, too.

# Introduction

WHEN YOU'RE SINGLE – and I mean seriously single (not just for a few weeks, or when you're 19 and making the most of being a commitment-free fresher at university) – life moves on a roller coaster of hormonal highs and crushing lows. Your world doesn't have the wonderful monotony of coupledom, where a modern girl knows that even if her man is dull, insensitive or a bit of a twat, at least he's *her* dull, insensitive twat – and she has someone to go on holiday with.

Being in a relationship is fabulous for this reason: security. If you've got a good man, you know that you have someone out there who is on your team. You have someone who puts you first, someone who loves you more than anyone else on earth. That's the aim, anyway – but if these things aren't met ... you know what? I'd take the highs and lows of singledom that I was talking about, instead.

I love being settled, I love having regular sex, someone to come home to and someone to look after, but when I've begun to feel used, abused and let down, I've made tough decisions to go it alone. Heck, I've left a marriage, and dissolved a live-in relationship in a strange city rather than feel second best. And I have never regretted either of those moves, because I know I deserve better, even if I'm having to make my own life better for myself.

Now, I'm in my early thirties, single and back in starting position when most of my friends are married mothers with mortgages – it's scary but liberating. I have times when being single has made me feel ten years younger and livelier than I felt even in the best moments of my previous relationships.

For the first time in my life I understand the importance of tree hugging, girl crushes, vibrators and eating chocolates in bed – it can get lonely out there without someone to cuddle. And you know what? I love it. I'm me – 100 per cent of the time. Being single means you can be selfish. You can put yourself first, not put your partner first. And in this busy world of demands – work, play, family and friends (plus getting to the gym and keeping up with Angelina Jolie's children) – it's good to do what you want to do once in a while. In a way, being single is like taking a break and having a look around you.

Of course, when you introduce dating, one-night stands and unrequited love into the life of a single girl, things get complicated. You can go from dreams to desire and to despair in 24 hours (gosh, I've been there!), and nothing is more upsetting. But I want this book to show you how to ride the storm of singledom, with your head held high, your self-esteem intact, and your resolve to lead the best life for YOU! To put you first.

Throughout this book, I encourage you to think, 'What do I want and what do I need?' Single life is fun, scary, sometimes lonely and often hard on the liver, but you'll get to know yourself – and to like yourself. Only then will you truly know who and what your future might hold.

Being single is not a curse; it's often a blessing!

# Chapter One

# Single state of mind

WE'VE ALL WATCHED the romantic comedies, read the slushy mushy chick-lit novels and lain in bed tearfully singing along to the latest love song on the radio. Life is about being in a couple – right? About finding the perfect person? About finding your other half, because you're not a whole human being if you're on your own – correct? Bugger! Why can't life always work out like a film, book or song? In real life, we're often on our own. We're single.

## Owners of a lonely heart?

We came into this life alone, and we die alone, so going through your adult years solo shouldn't be hard. But it can be. Whether it's the simple feeling of missing someone to hold you or just to hug you without saying anything (my number-one most-missed part when I'm not in a relationship), or whether it's someone to help you pay the mortgage, being single means putting yourself out there in the world more than when you are with a partner. Standing up for yourself, paying for yourself, organising yourself – and being your own cheerleader. Because apart from your mum – and we all need a supportive motherly figure in our lives – you need to be your own biggest fan. This will help you keep confident, strong and sane when you haven't got a partner to tell you how fabulous you are.

## Learning to communicate

A big problem for many single people is sharing their hopes and fears with their support network. We're not all super-confident and able to talk about ourselves easily. The best thing to do is to be honest with yourself and others – without being too self-pitying or miserable. Admit, 'Hey, it can be lonely' when asked, or say, 'Yes, I miss my ex-boyfriend,' but don't talk on and on because you're feeling uncomfortable. Only share what you wish to share, and don't get pushed into talking about sex (or the lack of it) if you don't want to.

## Offloading

We all need to let off steam, and without a significant other, us single folk need to find people we can trust so that we can offload to them. This can be difficult, because you don't want someone who will laugh at you – but you do want someone who will make you laugh. You want someone who's been there – but you don't want someone who is still there and will drag you down with her. Try to find someone supportive but realistic; someone who has experienced your plight but has now changed her life for the better.

---

**JEN, 31**

❝ The hell of being single, where do I start? You can't call your grandma without her asking if you've met a nice boy yet. "I'm 82, hurry up. Shall I introduce you to Flo's grandson?" My grandma is even trying to get me on Match.com. If it's not her, it's my friends, pitying me as if I'm a Bridget Jones clone: desperate and a bit man-crazy. The truth is I have my moments of desperation and craziness, but I'm loving it. My last break-up has taught me to paint, run, read, travel ... Positivity is key: people, places and actions. ❞

---

## Why are you single?

The biggest problem I've found when talking to other single modern girls is convincing them that there isn't anything wrong with them. Sadly, in these days of validation and insecurity (imposter syndrome, anyone?), we often judge ourselves on what we have, not on what we are. So, too often single girls think, 'Well if I haven't got a man, I can't be special, beautiful, lovely, wanted ...', the list goes on.

This isn't true. Please believe me. Don't waste a minute of your life with feelings of inferiority or shame. Sure, allow yourself to think, 'Bugger I'm wasting all the love and support and joy I can give, because I'm good as part of a couple,' but don't think you're not good because you're not in a couple. There are a very few things you need to change if you're single and blaming yourself. If any of the below apply, sort them out:

◆ Go out and look for your man – not scouting for boys with a determined, maniacal glare on your face. Just put yourself in the path of eligible men – in other words, if you don't want to be single anymore, don't hide away in your flat re-watching *The Hills* all weekend.

◆ Are you mean to men? Have you become a bit cynical and hard? Do you usher any potential love interest away before he's had time to win you over? Try a smile, try small talk, and try saying yes, not no all the time.

◆ Are you still in love with your ex? Is he all you can think and talk about? If so, other men will feel intimidated and put off. Let the ex go.

◆ Are you too fussy? Is no one good enough to deserve your time? You might come across as a cold-hearted snob. Even if this is just a persona you put out there to cover shyness or insecurity, it could turn dates off.

◆ I'm assuming your personal hygiene and grooming are perfect, so there's no weird aromas coming from you that will put people off at 20 paces.

So, there are a few things that you could improve to better your chances of finding a man, and we'll address them in the following chapters. But I have found that most people are single because:

◆ They've been dumped horrifically by their partner (AKA 'that stupid twat').

◆ They've had enough of their partner (AKA 'that selfish twat') and dumped him.

◆ They've come to a mutual decision that they're both too stupid and selfish to have a grown-up relationship, so they've called it a day together.

Being single in this day and age has little to do with minor physical flaws (as much as us girls would like to believe it's because we're a little bit fat) or personality traits. It's more likely to be a timing thing (you want commitment and he doesn't) or an another-bird thing (he's started fancying the new girl at work and you're suddenly the boring ball and chain). Or it's because you've given it a go and it's not really working, and one of you has decided to stop dragging it out before you make each other totally miserable.

As George Michael sang, 'I can't make you love me, if you don't.' Too true! This is why I truly believe it is better to be single and to get your kicks out of your girlfriends, career and a jar of Nutella than trying to convince yourself that things will change or improve drastically. They rarely, rarely do, I'm sad to say.

## The pressures of being single

In your twenties, often the greatest pressure comes from external factors: your mum demanding a son-in-law, your best friend wanting to be a bridesmaid, your best friend getting married herself and telling you to do the same, your school mates suddenly growing old overnight and demanding that to stay in the inner circle you must couple up, throw Jamie Oliver-inspired dinner parties and take weekend breaks together in Prague.

At some point in your twenties, most girls stop wanting to throw on their disco best and party, and turn for comfort in a Laura Ashley catalogue and a Saturday spent queuing in IKEA.

Looking back on my twenties (from my current standpoint as a single 32-year-old), I am amazed at what a hurry I was in, and why? I wanted the house, the posh crockery, the quiet comfort found in a routine of Tesco, B&Q and a dinner at friends' Victorian terraced homes. When I decided to get married I was 24 years old and my parents begged me not to do it, saying there was no need and that I should enjoy my career, my money, my friends, the world – and of course my boyfriend – but that I didn't need to make it official. Of course, as any self-respecting 20-something would do, I'm sure, when being bossed around by her parents, I cried, shouted and ultimately ignored them. My friends were settling down and getting hitched, I couldn't be the last to do so. I had an amazing wedding, and married a wonderful man – it just wasn't the right time for either. I know that now, of course, with hindsight. At the time, I just didn't want to be single. External pressures got to me.

## Your thirties

In your thirties, the greatest pressures are more internal. The biggest one, of course, for many of us (but not all) being that dreaded, hideous, most unfair of nature's curses: the biological clock. Being single and over 30 should actually be fabulous for us girls: we've just hit our sexual peak, plus we're more confident and know what we're doing (and what we should ask for) in the sack. Those biological and neurological factors combined should mean 30-plus modern girls should be having safe sex and outrageous orgasms whenever they want, enjoying their freedom and bodies with relish. But, instead, we're all too worried about the tick-tock, tick-tock of having babies. At this point, being single becomes less about finding the right man, and more about finding the right man to get you pregnant. There's nothing sexier than a man who talks about his godchildren and admires friends' babies. (Although, of course, modern guys know that this is a sure-fire way to make women weak at the knees and are using baby talk as get-your-knickers-off lines – and it works). Although many women don't want children, mainly I meet the ones who do. And in our thirties the fear factors usually spiral in the same three stages:

1. 'I really am enjoying life at the moment, my career is in a great place, I'm fit and healthy and happy, I love my home. In a few years, I'll need a man because I need to think about children.'

2. 'My career, yoga skills, and apartment aren't as important as my burning need to have babies very soon. Bugger! I need a man for that. I'll have to settle soon ...'

**3.** 'If I don't meet a man in the next 12 months, I'm going to the sperm bank. It's not really the man I want anyway, it's the babies.'

Then of course the other internal pressure us singletons put on ourselves in our thirties and forties is: are we going to die alone? Well, perhaps it's not as dramatic as that. But we certainly panic that we've got to stop having fun, being independent and working on our career, and just settle down and be sensible. I don't know whether it's just old-fashioned sexism or our innate need to nest, but around this age us modern girls start to feel guilty for being able to live on our own. We can be too capable, we muse, so perhaps we should tone it down and be a damsel in distress if we don't want to be single forever.

---

**NB Of course, the worst pressurisers in history are parents.** They don't necessarily love the cost of paying for a wedding, but they prefer that to the idea of having to explain that their daughter is single through choice/not a lesbian/ a brilliant, happy career girl. Parents are competitive and worry what their friends think about them. For your parents, every other child's wedding they have to attend will be like a dagger in their hearts. But it's not about them, it's about you, and we'll discuss how to handle them in Chapter 4.

---

## The wrong men at the wrong time

We've all been besotted by the wrong men at certain times in our lives. They won't be wrong for everyone. In fact it'll hit you like a punch in the stomach when you hear your ex who hated babies has got his new bird pregnant 12 months later. That's life, I'm afraid. It's all about timing and chemistry. Don't let this consume you – it's really not you or anything you did. But, whatever you do, don't get out your rose-tinted glasses and rewrite your relationship as something it wasn't. Learn from it – and from him – and let it help you decide how to improve your next man episode.

---

**DELAINA, 36**

❝ You can't live with a guy after a break-up. Get away. My mum always said, "They'll come back at some point," and they always do. One guy who dumped me hard called me six months later pretending it had never happened. Knowing he pined for me was an ego boost, but when I said, "Good luck with the rest of your life," he dragged his sorry ass straight into another relationship. When I found out he was engaged, I was a bit depressed – commitment was something we'd fought over – but I remembered all the reasons he was wrong for me. I was soon over it. ❞

---

## Getting rid of toxic men

I have witnessed too many fabulous laydeez being dragged down by bad boys. And I'm not talking about Colin Farrell or Robbie Williams-style bad boys – I'm talking about lazy, arrogant losers who feel secure enough to treat their partners badly. This is our fault, to a degree. More often than not, girls think about 'we'; whereas the worst kind of men just think about 'me'. Men can spot a pushover, and if the sex is good and they give good 'commitment' talk, we're suckers. Too often I've heard women justify staying in a bad relationship by saying, 'Well, he doesn't hit me and he's not unfaithful.' That's the very least you should expect! Some guys are just too awful to put up with them for reasons far less *serious* than these, and you should learn to recognise the signs and get yourself back on the single scene ASAP:

◆ He never calls or turns up when he says he will.

◆ He hasn't introduced you to any of his friends or family.

◆ He has never paid for anything!

◆ He climbs into bed in the middle of the night smelling of perfume.

◆ He has called you the wrong name, more than once.

◆ He puts you down, calls you nasty names or makes you miserable.

## Being brave and making changes

The world seems to be built for couples – and I'm not just talking about the holiday resorts of Sandals in the Caribbean, which will only allow you to stay if you're partnered up. No, more than that, the world is set up to encourage coupledom: everywhere you look, couples dine *à deux* in restaurants, go to the cinema together, argue at airports together. They might not be happy, but they're not alone.

This is what makes splitting up with someone so hard. Even when the warning bells are ringing in your ears louder than the historic chimes of Canterbury Cathedral, it's easier to ignore them and maintain the status quo than to disrupt everything and leave.

I'm not advocating running away at the first sign of trouble. You need to think hard, listen hard and change hard. You should go to joint counselling if you want to try to save the relationship. You should seek the opinions of those you trust, and ignore the gloating comments from those you don't. You should listen to your head and feel your heart. Only then, when you've tried and begged and wanted to change, should you walk away.

I've walked away from two very serious relationships and I was probably so determined and secure in my decision by the time I decided to walk, that other people – including the men – were shocked. Internally, however, I'd spent a year during both relationships questioning everything, asking myself why I was unhappy and crying so deeply and painfully that I would soak my pyjama top with tears of disappointment and dread – and guilt. Guilt that I wasn't happy and, because the men involved weren't brave enough to care, or bothered enough to change, that I had to be the 'baddie'. So, I had to call the shots, even though it hurt.

## A simple list

In both cases, when my marriage broke down, and when I knew I should no longer be with a live-in boyfriend, who I'd been dating for 18 months, I wrote a list. This sounds flippant and mechanical, but it worked. You see, after months of shameful sobbing and strange voices in your head screaming, 'Just be happy, just be happy! What do you expect real life is, you silly thing?' I was exhausted and confused.

Writing down the pros and cons of our relationship helped make my decision clear. In black and white it was obvious that however much the men wanted to ignore the issues, or I felt I should just put up and shut up, I couldn't. In black and white being single and happy was a better option than being coupled up and suffocated.

The list is just for your eyes. So write anything down – silly, small things or painful aspects of your relationship that have been slowly making you depressed. Then, of course, half the list should show the benefits of your relationship, what you love about your man, and what hopes you have for the future.

Here is a possible list of pros and cons, based on different relationships I have had:

| Pros | Cons |
| --- | --- |
| I fancy him | He doesn't want to have sex any more |
| He taught me to ski | He's not interested in my interests |
| He's got a great career | He thinks my career is silly and easy |
| I love his family | He doesn't love my family |
| Good sex | I come way down on his priority list |
| He looks good in his clothes | He forgets to call me |
| | He owes me money all the time |
| | He cuddles our cats more than me |
| | He doesn't look at me with love any more |

A list like this helped me to leave my last relationship. However hard it would be to be single again, at 31 in a big city, when all my friends were getting married and having babies, I had to do it. Staying in this sick relationship would have meant I had no self-esteem or dignity. Wouldn't I rather be on my own than with a man who – however much I adored him (and I did and always will in a way) – would walk in the house three hours late from work with no explanation and rush to our kittens and say, 'I love you, I missed you,' scooping them up in his arms and kissing them, while all I deserved was a sideways glance that said, 'Don't start.'

Being single is better than that, girls. No one deserves to feel worthless in their own home.

You may feel you are hiding bad relationships from the eyes of others, but those who know you well and care about your well-being will have known something was wrong and will support you. When I split up with the cat man, everyone – including my lovely, 82-year-old grandma, who thinks everyone is adorable – said, 'What took you so long?'

That was perfect. No one had interfered. They'd let me make my own decision. But they backed me 100 per cent once I had made my choice. He was adorable, but he was too young for me.

## The decision to divorce

Deciding to divorce is, of course, a much larger issue for everyone. Once you get a wedding certificate, the relationship stops being about two people and starts to belong to everyone: his family, your family, extended families, friends ... especially married friends who use your wedded bliss as justification for themselves staying in perhaps less-than-perfect relationships.

That's what shocked me most about suddenly becoming single again after five years of marriage. Not the legal dramas or the personal feelings of failure, or the worry that you were walking away from someone else's heart. I was most shocked by the hypocritical behaviour of some 'friends'. They were happy enough to come to Christmas parties and dinners, and to holiday together in the country – as long as we were all in couples. Suddenly single, I was dropped like a hot potato. Was I a threat? Were people suddenly jealous of my freedom? Did I highlight that things were wrong in their own relationships?

I hit my 'friendship' crisis point four months after separating from my husband. It was New Year's Eve and I was at a wedding of old school friends. My husband had decided not to go. (I said we could both go, or he could go and I would stay away, but playing his favourite role of martyr, he allowed me to go.) What a mistake. Weddings and New Year's Eves are emotional enough, but when you're alone and going through a divorce, they're hell. The added bonus was having old friends either (a) criticise me for leaving my husband when they knew nothing about what really went on (people rarely do); or (b) drunkenly slur that they hated their partners, and they were just with them for the time being or money (and did I have any tips?), while at midnight they would be kissing and grinning while

I downed a bottle of Veuve Clicquot and wondered why I'd made the effort to attend.

How do you get over this? Clear out the bad people; ignore the fools who don't understand because they've never been hit with relationship trauma. Instead, surround yourself with those who are true, kind and fair. I don't mean arse lickers who tell you what you want to hear. I mean people who truly love you.

## Getting over a divorce or serious relationship

This book isn't about divorce, or breaking up with people – it's about being single and getting your life back on the right track. But here are a few things I learned the hard way:

◆ Time is the best healer.

◆ Put yourself first.

◆ Don't rush into anything – or if you do, don't expect much from it. There's a reason why rebound relationships have such a bad name.

◆ Concentrate on your well-being: mental health (have therapy if you feel you need it, take up meditation or yoga, read books of encouragement, strengthen good friendships) and your physical health (don't turn to booze too often, but go to the gym and try a healthy diet to help your skin, hair and waistline).

◆ Get to know yourself again. Listen to yourself.

◆ Don't beat yourself up too much – there will always be someone out there willing to do it for you, and your ex is probably having a field day. You should remain your biggest fan.

◆ Know that however hard the decision was, it's made now, and from here you can only go onwards and upwards.

◆ Learn from your mistakes.

◆ Recognise what you don't want to recreate in your next relationship.

If it was his decision and you were thrown back into single-dom from a marriage you thought you were happy in, all of the above still applies. Just tell yourself this: if he couldn't see your value, or didn't love you as much as you deserved, then he's a fool and you're better off without him. Your family and true friends will tell you this, and you may think they're just saying what you want to hear. But it's true. One person cannot save a marriage. It takes two people to work hard to keep it alive. Even if you think you were faultless, there were probably things you could or should, or would have changed if you'd known it would lead to divorce. It's too late. Give yourself time, analyse yourself as much as you like, and be strong. This too shall pass.

## Your romantic recovery...

... starts the minute you become single again. Take a pledge: to enjoy yourself, to enjoy your friends, your money, and your family. It is scary. But I live by the motto that you should do something every day that scares you – it helps you to become the person you want to be and tests your limits. Be it as small as smiling at a stranger, or as big as going for a promotion at work. As the great Harold Macmillan (British politician and prime minister between 1957 and 1963) once said, 'To be alive at all involves some risk.' So being single involves some risk – good! It means you're alive. Getting out into the world as you, as a whole person, is exciting and liberating. People will notice you more – and, think about it, you get to have those first-kiss tingles and those first-shag sensations all over again.

## Secrets of success

◆ Whatever the circumstances behind your single status are, don't ever allow yourself to feel like a reject.

◆ When you're feeling down about being on your own, remember the grass is always greener on the other side. Your friends in relationships are probably jealous of your single status and all the freedom, lie-ins, nights out and romantic adventures it allows.

◆ Being single isn't all fun – I'm not pretending it is. When you feel alone, talk to your single friends (coupled-up ones will have forgotten the feelings being single brings). If you haven't got understanding friends around, buy the *Sex and the City* DVD boxed set and enjoy. Watching that show again as a singleton makes so much more sense – and makes me feel normal.

◆ So many people will feel that your sex life is up for discussion, but it's not if you don't want it to be. In fact, the more you keep private the better. Some people will judge you and that's just an extra pressure. Reveal info strictly on a need-to-know basis.

◆ Crying is fine. Put music on loudly so that your neighbours can be spared the wailing, and really get all the pain and hurt out there. A good cry really does help everything.

◆ If you're suddenly single and finding your new life difficult, take it slowly. But do know that single girls can go everywhere these days. I go on holiday on my own, to restaurants on my own, to the cinema on my own. You're not a leper – you're just single. And even if you feel you have 'single loser' tattooed on your forehead, no one else is paying any attention. That's the thing: everyone is so self-obsessed these days; we can all do what we want – alone or with someone else.

◆ Don't read all the scary articles about fertility nightmares and modern women running out of time to conceive. Lots of media outlets put out horror stories as some antiquated form of sexism, I'm sure, to take us modern girls out of the workplace. But it is something to think about, so do talk to your doctor if you have serious worries.

◆ Likewise, don't be scared if your biological clock is not ticking at all, let alone loudly. Many women don't think about children until they are in their late thirties – or they decide they never want children. This is all normal and acceptable. It's your life, you should make the choices that affect it.

◆ Buy a vibrator.

# Chapter Two

# Flying solo and living alone

F REDDIE MERCURY MADE 'Living on My Own (dee do de de)' sound like a constant disco with no time for monkey business. The truth is you will suddenly have lots more time on your hands – and it's wonderful. Suddenly all the time you have is for you. That means there'll be plenty of time for discos, monkey business and anything else you fancy.

## Who to live with

When you're a single modern girl, suddenly your domestic options open up and you can choose where to live and with whom. At a certain stage of coupledom, the inevitable move-in occurs and in a bid to be a good domestic partner, lots of your wants and needs go out of the window. I've lived with three men in my life and I know that the first thing to go is the remote control. Getting the television for an hour to watch my one favourite programme became such a battle that I would too regularly give in – and endure five hours of football.

## The benefits of living alone

Living alone sounds lonely – and of course it can be (who wants to watch Russell Brand on their own without someone to laugh with?), but most of the time it's friggin' brilliant. Just make sure you don't live somewhere too old and creepy that you can't get a proper night's sleep, and that you live in a female-friendly area; in other words not a house down a country lane or a flat accessible only from a dark alley. If you live somewhere safe with a good vibe, you're sorted.

Here are ten reasons why:

1. You can get up when you want – and you can definitely take a nap every Saturday afternoon without being kept awake by the sounds of rugby cheers in the living room. If you're hung-over, you venture into the kitchen for some marmite and toast before heading back to your sanctuary and a few more hours' kip without reproach.

2. You can eat what you want. No more will you have to pretend that you love meat with every meal, or that you won't get fat ordering in pizza at 10.00 p.m. because your man is a bit peckish. (Did you know women have to walk on a treadmill to burn the same amount of calories per minute as a man sitting on a sofa?) Life is cruel – but at least without a boyfriend leading you astray you have a hope in hell of staying trim.

3. Baths once again take their proper place as joyous, meditative experiences – not hurried get-clean dips. You can do the candles, the Take That album, a glass of vino … the whole biz. It's almost better than sex – and much less grubby.

4. Bedtime becomes something to look forward to. You can dive into clean sheets in your snuggly pyjamas, and read for as long as you like. There's no one to join you grumpily and demand the lamp is switched off, only to start snoring within minutes while your mind is still on the *Marie Claire* article you were wading through.

5. Your girlfriends can come over to discuss new men, good men, bad men, shoes, babies, Justin Timberlake and going to the Maldives, without getting evil glances. And, yes, you can wade through a whole packet of HobNobs and three cups of tea without any rude comments.

6. You can dance around in your underwear without feeling silly. A man might not love you jumping around to Mika's infectious 'Love Today', but it has to be done!

7. You can tweeze, squeeze, pick, groan and moan – and do other disgusting things us ladies shouldn't admit to, without fear of being caught. It's hard to keep up the feminine mystique when you're with someone 24/7.

8. It's perfectly acceptable to use the oven as shoe storage, to drape every hook with beads and bracelets, and to keep 12 different handbags out on display to keep your options open every morning.

9. Cushions and tea lights can play the central part of your interior design plans. And, as for flowers ... flowers can be everywhere and on everything: on curtains, in photo frames, fresh ones can be in vases in the bedroom. And there's no one to moan that it looks gay.

10. You can stay out all night and there's no one disapproving to come home to.

## Running your own home

If you do suddenly find yourself living solo, get your finances and goals in order as quickly as you can – but don't make any huge investment purchases until you've got to know the area, the place and how you want to live as a single girl living solo.

For two weeks I lived in my tiny apartment in Brooklyn with it completely empty before I knew what I wanted. How big a bed would I need when it was just me in it? Still quite a big one, I decided after a few days, because it was a great place to relax on Sundays with the Sunday papers and my copy of *1001 Buddhist Quotes*. How many photos would I want to hang up on the walls? After a few weeks I learned that in my lonelier moments I wanted to look around my little pad and be reminded of my happiest times and greatest holidays, so I hammered up clusters of photos of friends and family in every room. What colour should my furniture be and did I really need more than one sofa if it was just me? I was looking for peace and harmony, so I chose white (I didn't have to think about dirty trainers any more) and a deep, plush sofa that I could melt into for *Dirty Dancing* afternoons ... plus a few armchairs for when I hosted my first solo drinks parties.

When it comes to paying the bills, the easiest thing to do is to set up direct debits. And don't tack on extras like Internet service or 500 television channels until you've lived on your own for a bit and know if you would use them.

Don't go for something you can't afford. You don't want to have sleepless nights worrying about mortgage or rent payments. If you're determined to live in a certain area, don't compromise on location, compromise on size instead. You'll be amazed how modern girls can maximise space – and modern, single girls are rarely home anyway.

Befriend the nice next-door neighbours. An elderly lady and a strapping young man would be ideal – her to take in packages and share a slice of cake with, him to connect your DVD player. Introduce yourself in your first week in the new abode. It'll help you feel settled, and they can fill you in on the rest of the community, where the nearest swimming pool is, if the Chinese takeaway is decent, and so on. Once you get to know and trust someone, you can leave a spare key with them for emergencies – although a nearby parent or friend would be safer.

**NB The most important thing to do** when setting up home on your own is to make it all about you. My friends walked into my current apartment for the first time and loved it 'because it is so you!' Apparently the place with the boyfriend was all wrong, and, considering I'm quite a bossy, style-sensitive bird, it didn't reflect me at all. Just him. They loved that they felt at home straight away in my new apartment, because it felt like the home of someone they knew and loved. So don't hang on to old, shared possessions (my boyfriend kept the lot and gave me half the cash for it) and really indulge your own sensibilities. Don't do the place up for anyone other than you.

## Living with your parents

Lots of single girls won't have moved out of home, so they'll have to go through a break-up under their parents' noses. Don't share anything with them that you will regret later – especially if there's a chance you'll get back with the dude who let you go. Parents love the expression, 'You treat this place like a hotel,' while grimacing and moaning about how different things were in their day. They'll moan even if you pander around them like Cinderella, but try to limit their complaints, despite your post- break-up doldrums, by:

◆ Paying rent and buying your mum the occasional bunch of flowers.

◆ Cleaning up after yourself.

◆ Asking before bringing guests into their home.

- Not parading various one-night stands around in front of your dad.

- Keeping the music down.

- Not hogging the parking spaces.

- Saying thank you and spending quality time with them.

## Living with your parents – again!

If you're moving back in with your parents, all of the above applies too, of course, but returning to the nest has certain pluses and minuses. On the plus side, they'll probably be feeling a little sorry for you and the maternal instinct and paternal protection things will kick in; you'll probably get a good few breakfasts in bed and decadent Sunday roast dinners out of your misery, as well as the shocking return to your childhood bedroom. But, as well as the above, going home can make you feel really disappointed, as if you've regressed and let your adult self down. Don't worry about it. It's a chance to save money, eat lots of lovingly prepared vegetables and spend time with the people who probably love you more than anyone else in the world. When you really start regressing (fighting with your 17-year-old brother and grapevining in your bedroom to Bros), you need to get out. Run for the exit. Before that occurs, enjoy it and:

- If your old bedroom has been converted into a study, don't moan, go into the guest room with a smile on your face.

- Give your parents some sort of timeline – they've got their own lives now, so, as much as they love you, they might want to know whether this is a temporary situation or something a bit longer.

◆ Offer rent and insist they take it. And pay it when you say you will.

◆ Get the ground rules down. A lot could have changed since you were last under their roof.

◆ Don't use your dad as a taxi service. You're not 15 and stuck at the school disco any more.

◆ Be polite – you're now an adult, and half-guest, half-daughter. Don't just run yourself a bath and lock yourself in the bathroom for hours, or take what you fancy from the fridge without asking.

◆ Regain your front door key; otherwise you'll be waking the old folks up, you dirty stop out.

◆ Don't get frustrated if you get treated like a child. They can boss you around and moan about your clothes sense and you have to put up with it – sadly.

◆ Keep the swearing under control. You're under their roof now.

◆ Expect weekly comments about you being single, shelves and how you could well be left on one if you don't take relationships seriously soon – regardless of whose fault it is that you are in fact partnerless for a bit.

**CHARLOTTE,** 33

❦ I moved to Hong Kong with my boyfriend. He had a job offer he couldn't turn down and so I followed, stupidly selling my flat and leaving my career behind me. The pressure of being an ex-pat with nothing to do got to me, and within two years I was back in Blighty – and single. Shell-shocked and poor, my mum and dad welcomed me home with open arms. But it was almost too comforting. I became a child again and found myself turning down nights out to go back and watch the television with my parents. I had to snap myself out of it and move out before I became a total spinster. ❦

## How to live with your friends and stay friends

If only life were really like the cardboard set of *Friends*, and you and your friends were also a bunch of beautiful, wealthy, charismatic city slickers with a seemingly endless addiction to cappuccinos and teeth whitening. The reality will be something more like this: there will be nothing in the fridge (I mean, *you'll* have bought food, but in a pre-menstrual moment your pal will have eaten it all without replacing it), items of clothing will mysteriously go missing and then later show up back in your wardrobe smelling of cigarette smoke, and, perhaps worst of all, you'll have to listen to your pal getting it on through the wall when you're going through a shagging dry patch.

## Setting friend house rules

1. Before you move in, set up a house account so that shared expenses will be covered without surprises, fighting or shifty payment avoidance.

2. Hire a cleaner. Please! For the small amount it will cost to have someone in once a week, it will save a world of hassle and weekend arguments.

3. You may share a home, but you don't share anything else – without asking first. This goes for bottles of wine, toothpaste and men!

4. Don't invite anyone to stay over without checking first – I'm not talking about a man who is just in for 12 hours, I mean friends from Australia who want to kip in your lounge for a week. Having house guests is a pain in the arse, especially when they're not your guests – so always be considerate.

5. Don't let living together ruin the fun in your friendship. Make sure you still go out together and have a laugh. Don't treat each other like 'er indoors and only discuss the laundry.

## How living with friends can help you heal a lonely heart

The good thing about not going it alone is that you can't have too many solemn 'it's just li'l ol' me' moments. There will always be someone to gossip with over a glass of wine, and someone to ask how your day was. Living with a good girlfriend could actually be a more supportive situation than living with a self-centred boyfriend. She'll be someone to call if you're going to be late from work, and someone to share a Sunday-night Indian takeaway with. Good girl housemates can give you more laughs and home cooking than a lover – as for the other thing, that's what sex toys are for.

---

**NB If your housemate suddenly gets a boyfriend,** don't be overly jealous. Or even if you are jealous, try not to show it. Sure, moan to a trusted colleague at work who doesn't know your friend (so won't cause trouble), but try to be understanding. It can suddenly feel lonelier around the place, but you should be happy for her. Without being a bitch, tell her how you're feeling and make sure you slot special time in, just for the two of you. Go for a weekly manicure or something. If the new man starts spending too much time at your home, that's when you should have a word. It's not his place, and if he's going to be there often, he should start contributing.

---

## Group gaffs

So, living with one or two friends can provide the right amount of support – especially after a break-up when you need good people to pull you out of your slump. So what is living with a group like? Think Spice Girls circa 1996! Well, one good thing is that there will always be something going on. And even when you're mooning over your ex-boyfriend and happy to lurk around your bedroom listening to Celine

Dion, one of the group will make it their mission to drag you out to the pub. The house will have a permanent party vibe, as friends of friends descend on the house of fun. However, if you need time on your own, lots of sleep and a few months off drinking, living with a big group isn't the best idea. It'll probably be a happy house most of the time – but hectic. There are sure to be some fall outs. Limit your abode to three dwellers if you need your heart to recover in peace.

## Men behaving badly

You're a single girl; I can understand the appeal of living with a group of guys. At university, I lived with three rugby players. All my friends were soooo jealous ... until one of the guys drunkenly missed the toilet one night and pissed all over my fluffy bath towels. Living with men has its good and bad points:

Good:

They have hot friends – well, friends anyway.

Weirdos you accidentally give your home number to will soon stop calling.

Your mum will feel like you're being looked after.

There'll be plenty of naughty snacks available for PMT attacks.

They can sort out the DIY and electrics.

No one will steal your shoes or use your makeup.

Your girlfriends will always travel to you.

Bad:

Expect bad, loud rock music late at night when they return from the pub.

Weed smoking is considered acceptable.

There'll be no one to take emergency Tampax from.

You'll have to cover your magazine costs alone.

Sport: on the TV and as the main topic of conversation – constantly.

A house full of men could put off potential dates.

For them, cleanliness will be considered an over-rated virtue.

## A gay life

For many modern girls, the gay best friend is as important a part of life as Top Shop and *OK!* magazine. They are very good at providing the best of both sexes – makeup tips *and* an insight into the bluntness of the male species. Gay boys can seem like the answer to all our prayers, and they're so pretty and such fun they can easily fill the gap left behind by a smelly, emotionless ex-boyfriend. But be careful, darlings! The constant glamour offered by such delicious divas is great as a stopgap, but remember: (a) they won't marry you; and (b) they won't have children with you.

So go have fun and heal your heart, but don't surround yourself with only gay men. Single men will be intimidated and straight girls make better sharking partners when you're out looking for a new man. Live with your gay boyfriends for sure, but keep up with the girls. And don't be disappointed when you do start dating, and you find the straight guys sorely lacking in style, hygiene and humour. They're straight boys. They can't help it. But you love them anyway.

## Stranger danger

Suddenly becoming single when everyone else around you is happily shacked up can be traumatic, and if moving in with your family isn't an option and you haven't got enough cash to set up on your own, it can be even worse. You need to find yourself some roomies fast. Your safety and mental well-being are of utmost importance, so:

◆ Get recommendations from friends and family.

◆ Browse organised and regulated housemate websites.

◆ Meet your future live-in friends before you take the plunge.

◆ Get a house managed by a rental company, so that financial ramifications won't fall on you.

◆ Get a lock on your bedroom door.

◆ Give all your housemates' details to your mum and your friends once you move in.

◆ If you get a funny vibe after a while, move out. The only obligation you have is to yourself.

◆ Don't get overly friendly too quickly. Keep your own friends, and don't introduce the housemates to everyone you ever meet immediately. You should keep some things separate.

♦ Try not to sleep with the new boy you've just moved in with – it could make mornings around the kettle very awkward. Give it a few months to see if there really is something there, not just drunken loneliness.

## Money matters

Everyone I ask says they seem to become more financially stable when they're single. Without knowing it, you've been shelling out for your man half the time – for little pressies, covering his rent for a few months, or even eating more takeaways than you would on your own. Still, as soon as you know what your housing costs will be, look at what is left of your salary – and perhaps, in this time of mental insecurity, it would be sensible to start saving or investing in a pension. This will give you peace of mind when Prince Charming isn't riding into your life to make your future all rosy for you. Take control. It's empowering to know where your cash is going and that you'll always be OK. If you're not used to making big decisions solo, talk to your company's human resources manager for advice, or your bank's financial advisor.

## Making the most of your new home

This is all about embracing the selfishness that comes from not living with a partner – enjoy it! Yes, if you're living with others, you have to be kind and considerate, but no one has that Uri Gellar-like control of your brain that will turn you into a doormat. You are no longer a puppet to anyone's whims. Get up when you want to, go to bed when you want, stay out when you want. I never, ever thought I'd think this (hence my hanging around in a relationship with a guy who was emotionally killing me for six months longer than he should have been allowed to), but living alone as a modern, single girl is wonderful. I smile walking into my apartment, I smile walking down my new street. It's mine, all mine – and my place is always the same when I get in from work as it was when I left it.

---

**JACQUI, 32**

 After four years with Tom, I finally left him. I signed a new lease and packed my stuff. The movers came two hours early and Tom awoke to the men banging on our door. In a scurry of boxes and tape, Tom lay in bed weeping, as the movers moved my life out of our apartment. He was supposed to be at work – he wasn't meant to see this. It took ten minutes and all the evidence of my four years with him was gone. Tom was left with just a few traces – my hair on his brush, a few cookie crumbs in the oven. I completely destroyed him and I sometimes wonder, "When is karma gonna come and bite me on the ass?" But it hasn't yet, and I'm now happy to go home every night.

## Secrets of success

◆ Don't buy a full-on dinner service. Chances are you won't be doing a Nigella when you live on your own, a set of china and cutlery for two or four should do it. And if you're living with a gang, you won't want to buy anything too decent in case it gets broken.

◆ Use your new time wisely – use your new home to turn over a new leaf. Join a local gym or swimming pool, and see what classes the local college has to offer.

◆ Don't be persuaded to live with a friend who annoys you in small doses. Having to cope with large, live-in doses will drive you nuts.

◆ Don't cover someone else's rent. You might have trouble getting it back. It's always good to have a property manager to take care of finances – because money does ruin relationships, even family ones!

◆ Keep the numbers of local taxi firms in your mobile phone in case of emergencies.

◆ Even if you get back together with an ex live-in partner, don't rush to move straight back in together. It obviously didn't work before, so take things slowly.

◆ Even if your new home is smaller than the one you shared with an ex, it's all yours. Don't feel like you've taken a step down – it's a step towards finding (and living with) the real you.

# Chapter Three

# Entertaining yourself

S PARE TIME AND SELFISH pursuits are a godsend in these stressful times. So when you're not having to think about your boss or your mum or your best friend's wedding, enjoy singledom and all the fun and freedom it brings. Amusing yourself is so much easier than you think. In fact, after a little while of being single, you'll learn things about yourself and what you like to do – and you'll be able to take this new education into your next, healthier relationship.

## How to keep yourself busy

The shock of not being with your partner every spare moment of the day can seem daunting. But, actually, it's rather fab. You no longer have to go to his awful family's for a Sunday roast – you can spend your whole quota of family time with the family you really love: yours! Suddenly, if you're going to have a late night and get drunk (and therefore have a hellish time in the office the next day), it can be because you boozed and boogied with your mates, not because he forced you to drink too much Guinness in front of the television while watching a Ricky Gervais DVD. And then, of course, the biggest bonus is not wasting time waiting for him: hanging around for him to call, to come home, to arrive at a restaurant, to come to bed … Oh no, you're now in control of the clock. You will notice you can do so much more with your weekends and evenings. This is wonderful, although I can understand why you would be nervous about keeping busy to start with. Try the following:

◆ **Start a fabulous beauty regime.** A weekly schedule of pedicures, manicures and massages. You'll look forward to it all week.

- **Get fit.** Instead of being a couch potato with your ex, you can be a triathlete with your spirit intact.

- **That thing you've always said you wanted to do?** Do it. Don't procrastinate. Transfer all the time you spent worrying about your man, to time worrying about learning those Italian phrases for your beginner's class.

- **Pick up old friendships.** Email or Facebook friends from the past and catch up on your lives.

- **Start new friendships.** That girl in your building that you enjoy chatting to in the car park. Ask her round for a glass of wine one evening.

- **Take out a magazine subscription,** or even get a newspaper delivered every morning. You'll always look forward to its arrival – and you'll educate yourself at the same time (this'll be handy for conversation starters when you're dating).

- **Start a reading group** or a film club.

- **Get brunching.** Arrange to meet other fabulous single girls every Sunday at midday. Have it in a regular place so that you get to know the staff and feel comfortable getting there early, and just showing up to eat feels normal.

- **Tick off your life's to-do list.** You know all those pesky, nagging chores that have been hanging around and you've never found the time? Well, now the time's found you. Print out all your photos from your digital camera and put them in an album.

- **Update your iPod.** Start a diary. Start a birthday book and address book. Go on the Web and research the ten places you most want to visit in the world and make mini destination folders. Write a novel.

♦ **Sleep.** Get your pyjamas on; coat yourself in unbecoming beauty creams and whitening toothpaste. Wear those moisturising mittens and slippers to bed. And tuck yourself up and take care of yourself. You'll look radiant on the outside – and sleep helps stress and depression.

## Enjoy the silence

Life is noisy. One unrecognised joy of being single is the stillness of mind it can bring. Get used to the quietness of being alone. Get yourself a book list, go and buy a collection of novels you've always wanted to read and indulge yourself at weekends. We've become too overstimulated, always needing the television or the radio on, or to be on the phone to friends. Rediscover your favourite books and find new authors that write about what you like. When I recently became single again, I learned simple relaxation and meditation techniques. It worked for me. I would look forward to having a bubble bath, then sitting on the floor, forgetting about my day and remembering the things I loved in peace and quiet. Without forcing anything, hopes, plans and dreams will flood your head and help you to discover what you need in a relationship.

## Motivational music

I always find that playing the right song can put you in a good mood and give you the lift to keep you energised for life – be it just getting up for a jog in the morning before work, or to build up your confidence before a night out on the singles market.

Enjoy that it's just what you want playing in the car or in

the house. No more nights of Pink Floyd! Embrace it. Dig out your teenage faves, and explore new music that gets great reviews in your favourite magazines. The world is a much better place when you're singing in the shower and dancing in your slippers. It's cheap therapy.

## TOP TEN ENERGISERS

The following have worked wonders when I've needed to embrace my solo status:

'Go Your Own Way' by Fleetwood Mac

'Someone Saved My Life Tonight' by Elton John

'Wanted' by The Cranberries

'Put Your Records on' by Corrine Bailey Rae

'Unwritten' by Natasha Bedingfield

'Song for a Friend' by Jason Mraz

'Shine' by Take That

'Snowflakes' by Just Jack

'Take on Me' by A-ha

'Don't Rain on My Parade' (from *Funny Girl*) by Barbra Streisand

## Doing things on your own

When you're used to being in a partnership, even walking into a bar to meet friends on your own can be intimidating. You feel like everyone is looking at you and you feel so self-conscious it would be easier to hide away. Well, the good news is – no one cares! Everyone is far too busy feeling self-conscious themselves. No one is looking at you, or thinking, 'Why is that girl on her own?' (Unless it's a guy who has spotted you and is planning on moving in for the kill: in his case, he's hoping you are on your own.)

But it's still difficult. The first time I went to the cinema on my own I felt most peculiar. I ran in at the last minute, without stopping for my usual quota of extra-large cola and extra-large popcorn. I sat in the middle (not in the back row certainly – there would be no snogging for me, thank you) and ran out as the film ended. But during the film? I forgot I was alone. In fact, one of my ex's tricks was to look at his phone during films, so it was a delight to be without that distraction. And what I did notice: there were lots of people in there on their own. I wasn't alone.

---

**NB If you're a bit nervous about going to the cinema** the first time, cheat. Go with another single friend but sit on your own. Meet afterwards for a cocktail and discussion. You'll soon notice all the other loners in your faux-alone state. If that seems too contrived but you're still nervous, just head to a chick flick. I assure you there'll be lots of birds in there alone. Men will not allow themselves to be dragged along for a weepy love-fest.

### TIPS TO STOP FEELING NERVOUS OUT AND ABOUT ALONE

**1.** Always have a book or magazine on you to pass the time.

**2.** Have an iPod on you to escape into your own world if you're nervous.

**3.** Use your phone or Blackberry to text friends for support.

**4.** Smile at strangers. If in a restaurant, start a conversation with the staff. They'll welcome some small talk – it's an improvement on rude customers!

**5.** Remember business professionals the world over are out eating, drinking, partying, and so on, on their own every day. Learn how to network better.

When you're single and solo, you are so much more open to life, and so much more approachable. I've met four times the amount of cool people while being single that I did when I was in a couple because I'm so much more aware of others around me.

### TIPS FOR GOING TO A PARTY ALONE

**1.** Get talking to some ladies in the loos and they'll take you under their wing.

**2.** Don't get drunk. You may think it gives you confidence and a certain *je ne sais quoi* but it doesn't. You stop being the girl on her own and become the drunken mess on her own.

**3.** Arrive early and leave early. This way you can spot good people as they arrive and you'll get a chance to talk, and then leave before you start to feel like a cling-on.

### JULIE, 29

❝ There's so much to do; I don't know how anyone is ever bored, or has time for a demanding man. Learn to love to read, write, paint, run ... learn new things, new hobbies. The more you do, the more people you will meet and the more things you will know. Sure, sometimes I feel like hiding from a world full of couples. So I order in a Chinese, and eat it straight out of the containers – and I'm not worried if I've eaten all the baby sweetcorns or if I go back for seconds and thirds. ❞

## Life skills

Being single really is the best time to educate yourself, because you have the time to study, and there's no one to stare at you resentfully when you're tucked up in bed with textbooks. Take the time now while you have it to help build your future:

◆ **Try languages.** Learn the native tongue of somewhere you often travel to, or would like to go to in the future.

◆ **Learn house skills.** Gardening, cooking, car maintenance, basic DIY ... you'll be even more eligible with these talents.

- ◆ **Help yourself get that promotion** by learning more about your industry, computers, confidence skills, and so on.

- ◆ **Learn skills for a new profession.** Has this new phase in your life prompted you to look at other areas of your life? Is your career one of them? Now is the time to learn skills that could help you move into a new profession – anything from photography to plumbing is taught part-time at local colleges.

- ◆ **Attend seminars and lectures on modern romance and dating.** Don't be embarrassed to learn more about men, and your relationships with them.

## Who to have around you

Modern girls leading a fulfilling single life need an array of good, positive people around them. The most important group is, of course, other single girls, not only to go out on the pull with but also to stop us from feeling like freaks. More about these valuable characters in Chapter 6.

Single girls also need to have non-smug married types around, to remind them that relationships can be healthy – and to introduce them to like-minded single boys. Friends' husbands and boyfriends are very useful for this purpose. They can also give you a boy's perspective on stuff without being mean or threatening.

Single boyfriends are also useful. They can give a much-needed confidence boost when times are tough – but make sure they tell you the truth (and tell you your plus points, of course). My best boyfriend and I had a really jokey relationship, full of lots of brother-and-sister-style teasing about bad outfits and brain meltdowns. However, when I became single and started to feel a bit vulnerable, his joking got too much. But rather than sulk in silence I sat him down and admitted, 'I'm feeling touchy – can you be gentler with me?' Since then it's been compliments and cuddles. And he's the first person I go to for advice when a new man is on the scene, and vice versa. With friends, honesty is good. And sensitivity is even better.

If you're lucky enough to have a good family, rely on them for a bit. Regress into the comfy world of childhood. If you fear they'll be judgemental, though, steer clear. This is your life. They can't live it vicariously through you, and their disappointment is not needed now.

---

**CLARE,** 36

❛ I went through a horrific break-up with my fiancé, from which I think my heart will never recover. For the first six months I stayed in, shell-shocked and scared about the future. Then, quite by chance, I kept bumping into a girl I used to work with at my local Starbucks. We chatted and I found that she'd split from her man the same week I had – but she'd pulled herself up and dusted herself off quicker than I had. Very soon, she wouldn't let me stay home at weekends; she'd ring me and make me come out. I'd forgotten how much I loved to go out and dance, until I met her. Now, even though it's not the same as being with Jack, I look forward to weekends and the music. ❜

---

## Lonely nights

It's amazing how you can be out and about, busy and fulfilled, then you shut your front door, throw your bag on the floor – and you're on your own. And that's when it hits.

The loneliness. The crushing realisation that for the next ten hours or so it's just you and your duvet, and, if you're lucky, a few Jo Malone candles. Sadly, there's not a magic cure for this; you just have to embrace it. Lock the door, pull on your nicest jimjams and admit defeat – you can keep your sexy underwear in the drawer for the night.

I've learned to enjoy my nights in on my own so much now that I have to force myself to go out. When work is tiring – and especially on the evenings from November until March – I can happily spend each weeknight in with my television, BBC podcasts and takeaway deliveries. Embrace rambling around your place doing chores (your laundry can provide a massive distraction, as can colour-coordinating your wardrobe, which are both also very useful things to do) and walking around naked. Now is the time (because you've got the time) to start tweezing your bikini line and learning to do your own pedicure.

What not to do when you're lonely: give up instantly! It takes time to get used to it – don't give in after a few weeks and move in with your parents or return to your ex just because you're a bit bored or scared. For calmness of mind, there's nothing nicer than living on your own. Get a cat, a secure lock and don't move into a home without a bath.

---

### YOUR EMERGENCY LONELY NIGHT KIT

- A pile of magazines and Sunday supplements you never got round to reading.

- *Lace*, *Thornbirds* and *Valley of the Dolls* paperbacks.

- Molton Brown bubble bath and self-heating face packs.

➡

- Häagen-Dazs in the freezer and Oreo cookies in the fridge.

- Unseen episodes of anything featuring Russell Brand, Jonathan Ross or Ant and Dec.

- Fleece blankets and cushions, and soft slipper socks.

- Nocturnal friends' numbers on speed dial.

**NB It's OK to stay in on a Friday night** with a microwave meal for one. Who cares? If you need a night in, or can't be bothered to drag your sorry arse to some hideous event with hideous people, embrace staying in. I'd rather be in watching *Miss Marple* on the most social night of the week than queuing in the cold to pay over the odds for a sickly cocktail. The coolest girls I know hibernate on Fridays and Saturdays, exhausted by their Monday to Friday of hard work, tough workouts and commuting. It makes getting up for yoga on Saturday mornings so much easier too. If you're worried that sounds desperately uncool, remember what Edith Wharton said in *The Age of Innocence* about the Van der Linden family, who made themselves all the more socially desirable because they did not go to the opening of a fridge door! They saved themselves for only the best nights out, and therefore everyone fought to include them in the best events.

# Long weekends

I'm not talking about long weekends at Easter; I'm talking about Friday nights to Monday mornings when you feel friendless and socially inadequate. This is the hardest thing I've found about being single: when you're part of a couple you don't even have to think about how to spend your spare time. As a woman, more often that not you're waiting around for your man or falling in with his demands (watching football, going to a DIY store, chatting to his mates' tarty new girlfriends).

Suddenly, without a couple's weekend routine to fall into, you have to make an effort. If you don't, you could find yourself on your own and not talking to anyone for 48 hours. So keep yourself entertained over the weekend by:

◆ **Planning ahead.** Book beauty treatments and cinema tickets.

◆ **Taking on a big project.** Commit to exploring a new area or helping a friend move, or gather a group of similarly single fab girls to have brunch with on both Saturday and Sunday – this will break up your days.

◆ **Not being shy.** Be honest – tell people you're lonely. On my first aimless weekend as a single girl, I texted a friend to ask, 'What do I do?' He rang me straight back, admitted weekends were the hardest thing for single peeps like us, and insisted we go on a bike ride. I would never normally do this, but I loved it – so be open to ideas. Say yes to every invitation.

◆ **Email people on Friday** to say you're around and can they keep you in the loop.

◆ **Score brownie points** (you'll need a stash later, when

you've got a new man and he's taking up all your time) and visit your granny or offer to babysit your godchildren.

◆ **Take control.** Invite people over to yours for a dinner party or girls' night in.

---

**5 TIPS FOR GOING TO AN EVENT SOLO**

What's a girl to do if you're determined to go out but your close buddies are busy? Answer: go anyway. Here are five top tips to take entering a room alone in your stride:

**1.** Dress yourself up, blow out your hair, and spritz your favourite fragrance on your pulse points. Looking and feeling sexy will give you confidence.

**2.** Head for the host and say you're shy and friendless and ask if there's anyone you should meet. The host will think it's fab you made the effort to come.

**3.** Hang out near the drinks or food areas.

**4.** Go to an event with some conversation-starter ideas – read the newspaper or check out perezhilton.com before you leave the house.

**5.** Smile, and look helpless – people will come to your aid.

---

## Travelling alone

It's too easy to put off going on holiday if you haven't got a partner. Your family would be on your nerves if you were with them for longer than three days, your friends are busy with their own love lives, and there's not a man out there to whisk you off into the horizon.

Well, the good news is that more and more women are travelling alone now. Don't feel embarrassed to go into your local travel agent to discuss your options, and go on the Web and check out accredited travel Internet sites. A sure-fire way to go somewhere with other like-minded women is to go to a themed resort. I have just booked to go on a week-long bikini boot camp in Mexico. I googled two words: yoga and beach, and it came up with a fabulous place. A quick phone call to the owner confirmed it was just what I needed: a small, boutique, beachside retreat that specialised in silent morning shore runs, meditation and spa treatments. I booked immediately. When I started telling friends, a few hinted to join me and, much to my surprise, I said no, I want to do this on my own. I needed peace and quiet to meet people removed from my everyday life. The flight might be a bore, but hey, I've got my laptop and iPod. If a long week away seems too much, see if you can cope with travelling alone by going somewhere nearby for just two nights. I went to Austin, Texas, for a weekend as my trial run – and the great thing I noticed was that hotels are full of solo travellers, and when you're abroad, it's so easy to get talking to new people. A different accent is the best ice-breaker in the world.

You should actually relish the opportunities we have to travel these days: we have money, flights and freedom – just beware of your carbon footprint. I will never wait for someone to agree to tag along with me again. When I think back to all the offers of villas, and so on, I turned down in the past because my exes didn't fancy it, I feel mad at myself. The greatest gift we can give ourselves is to see the world and get to know its people. Don't let a stupid man or busy friends get in the way.

## Secrets of success

◆ Make the most of this 'just you' time to make a 'better you': concentrate less on negative feelings of loneliness and boredom and more on things like working harder to get a promotion, working harder to get a better body, and working harder to build the friendship circle you've always wanted.

◆ If you're feeling a little lonely, feel free to text, email or instant-message friends. Get all 'high school' and gossip to keep yourselves amused, without having to leave your house or ask for invitations.

◆ However desperate you are for company, don't bolster failing friendships that you know are wrong or unhealthy. Start fresh with friends too, while you're starting fresh with your romantic life. Some weirdos will sense your vulnerability and make a play for you.

◆ At this difficult, sometimes lonely, time in your life, some new people will appear like guardian angels. Perfect! Have fun with these newcomers and get their perspectives on your old situation, then embrace the new opportunities they offer you — be it going to new bars, meeting new men, or trying new plays at the theatre.

◆ Love yourself, and love being by yourself. When you've got kids, you'll wonder how you ever felt low about having time on your hands.

# Chapter Four

# How others view the single girl

W HEN YOU BECOME SINGLE, you're too busy thinking about your new life and your next steps to
think too much about what other people are
thinking about, but believe me they are thinking – and it's
often about you. Here's how to handle the interfering irri-
tants and the nosey know-alls.

## Perceptions of the single girl

We tend to fall into three stereotypes:

**1.** The desperate, needy romantic.

**2.** The independent lady with a cat.

**3.** The shag monster.

Now, I've been all three and continue to fluctuate between
them from week to week – minus the cat (the ex-boyfriend's
got that!). As true as these modern-girl characteristics can be,
we all have deeper feelings and needs than these and it's going
to get annoying when others stand around discussing your
love life – or lack of it – with a nudge, nudge, wink, wink.

### The desperate, needy romantic

Some women who are in relationships like to think that
their single sisters all fall into this first type. That instead
of embracing single life, we're in every night, crying and
praying for Prince Charming, and sticking up posters of
George Clooney, dreaming that one day he'll fall in love
with us. I was that person for a while. When I first split up
with my husband, I didn't know what to do. I had been in a

relationship for eight years, and although it wasn't right for me to be married, I did like the security that a partner brought to me.

Of course, my coupled-up friends tried to tell me that I should settle, and that being lonely in a relationship was better than starting again on my own. Any time I cried, or felt a bit needy, or showed any signs of being desperately unhappy, they kind of enjoyed it. Isn't that terrible? But you soon learn that people often stay in relationships that they aren't so happy in – and your bravery and standing alone will highlight their own failings. They need to think you're desperate and needy to get on with their own troubled relationship. Figure this out as soon as you can. They're not healthy people to be around. Even if they pretend to be friends and to be looking out for you, their stuff will get in the way and you won't ever leave a meeting with them feeling good about yourself or your situation. It's hard luck that at this difficult time in your life, you have to learn who your real friends are too, but it will be worth it in the long run. I've cleared out the time-wasters and now have a life filled with amazing, true friends. My divorce taught me that.

Becoming this needy stereotype certainly got me into a new relationship quicker than was really healthy. So it's no surprise that didn't work out.

## The independent lady – cat or no cat

When I split from my boyfriend, two years after the ghastly separation from my husband, I'd learned a few lessons. I also had an amazing group of people around me, who loved me and agreed with my decision. Most people in my life had assumed this had been a rebound relationship, and advised me to just step back from men for a bit, to give myself time to recover from both heartbreaks. They thought I should be independent for a while, to get to know who I really was – after all, I'd given everything to the men in my life for ten years now, and had never really thought about what I wanted since I was 22 years old. It was sound advice.

For a good few months, I stayed in and spent time in my gorgeous – tiny – apartment, which was all mine. I listened to and watched what I wanted to, I spent time writing and reading, and eating girly foods for dinner like hummus and carrots. Sometimes I didn't want dinner at all – just Minstrels, so I did that too. For three months, I allowed myself to have whatever I wanted. Some times, I'd go to the gym every day, other weeks I avoided it like the plague. But this time when I hid from my tracksuit, I didn't have anyone telling me I 'was getting old and fat', as my ex-boyfriend used to tell me. Oh no, I only had myself to answer to and I knew I wasn't lazy, so I must have been tired and allowed myself time off.

Independence is great: living in a big city at this time, I finally got to go to museums and galleries (I'd been asking my ex to go with me for ages but he never fancied it), and when friends asked me to go to the tennis championships or abroad for a holiday, I could decide if I wanted to spend *my money* and give up *my time* and make the right decision for *me*.

Every single girl needs this time to regroup: to decide where things have gone wrong, accept her part of the blame and heal properly before attempting to do it all again. Surround yourself with good people and enjoy the selfishness of independence. Just don't become so hardened and self-serving that a new relationship will seem (a) a drag; or (b) impossibly demanding. Stand on your own two feet while remembering the companionship and loyalty a healthy love affair can bring.

The people around you who love you will feel so proud and give you many a pat on the back. If you feel lonely during this time, be honest. Tell your family and your best friends that you need cuddles and attention. They'll give them to you.

## The shag monster

This is possibly the most fun stereotype. It's interesting that once you become single, people – even strangers – will feel your love life (and particularly your sex life) is fair play for dinner-party discussions and comments over coffee. The single girl enjoying her body, you see, will incur lots of jealousy and resentment from people around her. So your good friends will live vicariously through you and will want to know every detail, whereas others who aren't getting any and are a bit miserable in general, will want to look down on you to make themselves feel superior. What sad beeatches!

After a few months of being single and sorting out my head, I decided to get out there and have a bit of fun in the man department. I've always believed that as long as you're healthy (use a condom) and happy about it (don't confuse sex with love), a modern girl has as much right to have an interesting and fulfilling, er, night life, as any man. So I embarked on a period of flirting, kissing, saucy texting and occasional hook-ups. Good for me, I thought. Good for you, thought my good friends. My parents? Gosh, I didn't tell them about the newly liberated me, of course.

For my married-with-kids mates, I'd send email updates and they'd send back encouragement and demand to see photos of the new beaux. They all loved it and I loved getting their feedback. Only trust good, true, non-gossiping pals with these updates. You don't want to start rumours or judgements. Certainly don't feel you have to disclose anything you might regret. Coyness is good.

## Keeping private stuff private

When randoms ask you about your sex life – colleagues, friends of friends, men in bars – stay shtum. You don't need to answer anything. Being a single girl, everyone feels they can offer an opinion or advice. If you don't disclose anything, you'll stop this kind of interference in its tracks. It's fun to tell silly, shagging anecdotes to a crowd, but resist it. I have too often become a clown and shared too much about 'the man who never called me back', in a bid to hide my own insecurity or worry. But when the laughing stopped, and I went home alone, I always berated myself for being so open. Don't feel the need to become other people's idea of what a single girl having fun is – just be your own idea of fun.

---

### KATIE, 29

❝ My hairdresser recently found out that I was 29 – and single! She then asked if I was thinking of having my eggs frozen. So even if I couldn't hear the click of my biological clock, other people think they can, and throw lots of desperate and needy feelings at my feet. Single male friends of mine have been convinced that they couldn't hear what women over 30 have been saying on dates because their clocks are ticking so loudly. Why does everyone feel the need to make assumptions about us single girls? ❞

# The lesbian thing

Nothing against lesbians – whatever floats your boat – but if you're a single, straight woman over 30, some people assume that you're waiting for the perfect woman, and it gets a bit annoying. I hear it about people all the time. If a celebrity female hasn't got a fella and she's a few years from 40, that's it – she's batting for the other team and that's how society will label her. It's the same for us muggles. This is annoying for a few reasons:

◆ It highlights how limited society still is to the woman *left on the shelf*. At no point is she exalted for not settling, earning her own money or having a great career. It's down to this: if she hasn't got a man, there must be something wrong with her. Or she likes the ladies and is afraid to come out. However, I've never known this to be the case. The lesbians I know are out and proud, and more often than not, having much better relationships than the couples I know!

◆ It turns your single status into a bit of a joke. After a few months of being single, my straight bloke friends started suggesting I try the girl-on-girl thang. I became some kind of freak and they found the idea of me having a lesbian fling either sexy or funny.

These stupid men, or strangers, who question our sexuality, raise an annoying point: if only we were lesbians! If you're still single in your thirties you've probably come across enough men to feel disappointed with most of them. I meet amazing women every week and I get crushes on them – I want to hear what they have to say, they look great, they're interested in my opinion, we got out and have a laugh … we just don't fancy each other. We fancy men. Life sucks.

Just ignore it all! Some men are perverts trying to fulfil some fantasy, and women who are in dull, serious relationships want to think you're hiding something, instead of believing you're just holding out for a hero. My ex-husband even tried to allude to me being a lesbian because I didn't want him. If I wasn't prepared to put up with him, I must want a woman, right? Wrong! Just ignore the silliness and do what makes you happy.

## How to handle the friends who have more than you

It's easy to slip into a downward spiral of jealousy and resentment for the people around you who have the conventional ideal of happy adulthood sorted out: husband, 2.4 children and a nice house with a garden. Don't do it. Jealousy is a horrid thing.

1. Don't just look at your worth in terms of whether or not you have a man (a trap many women fall into). Look at every aspect of your life and personality. Someone else may have a husband, but you have a great job, a cool car, many friends, a great holiday booked, and so on.

2. Talk to your friends and family. Learn from them. How did they like being single, what do they miss, do they ever get frustrated or lonely? I bet you their answers will make you feel better about your life.

3. This too shall pass. Don't look at your life in black and white. Where you are in your life now – being single – isn't for forever. It could change in a month, or a year. The great thing about being single is that you're not tied to anyone, and anything can happen. Embrace the freedom, knowing that good things are around the corner.

4. Don't look at being single as a character flaw. It's a lottery who gets coupled up or makes those coupledoms last. Young, old, fat, thin, saint or sinner – it's all random. Never believe you are single because you are ugly, boring or unwanted. There really is someone out there for everyone. In fact, there are multiple people out there for everyone. It's all about timing.

5. If you feel yourself getting jealous of what certain couples around you have, direct it in a healthy manner. The couple whose relationship you admire? Ask them to fix you up with someone suitable, or to give you advice on settling down with the right person.

---

**DEBI, 33**

❝ When you've been single for as long as I have, you start to have unrealistic ideas of what it's like to be in a relationship. The friend who has the husband, house and children is usually run ragged with no time for herself or girly nights out. Listen to her! Listen to the details of her life! The husband you're so envious of picks his feet in bed, dismisses her opinion and comes home drunk after work parties and demands sex. She'll wistfully remember the days you're having now: shopping for shoes and not having to justify it to anyone. Support each other and share the best and the worst, and you'll both feel happier. ❞

## Jealous girlfriends

Ooh, when people are jealous of you it's not easier. That's when you find out who your friends are, and where your frenemies live. Some wise old dude said, 'Keep your friends close, and your enemies closer.' He wasn't that wise. Tell 'em to clear off. Obviously, some people are jealous of you for personal reasons that you should be sympathetic to and try to help them out with: loneliness, a sense of failure or disappointment with their own life, a cruel partner that they wish they had the courage to leave. These are all tough obstacles to overcome, and their jealousy is directed towards you because they feel you've been strong where they are weak. In a way, it's a compliment. Keep that thought in the back of your head and work with them to highlight your fears – show them your life is not perfect, but it's what you've got, so you're going to live it in the happiest, healthiest way you can.

Your kindness and openness can only go so far with jealous friends though. Some people are just bitter, mean and nasty. And at certain key moments in your life, they will reveal themselves. As I've mentioned, when I got divorced a few nasty characters (who I always had an inkling about) showed themselves to be back-stabbers, gossips, liars and misogynists – even the women! These types are jealous of your new freedom as a singleton, they'll be jealous when you get a nice new man; hey, they'd be jealous if you came out of the closet and you got a lot of attention! They're not happy with themselves so they can't be happy for anyone else. Try to be nice to them but don't make a mug of yourself, and walk away with a lightness of heart when you've given all you should.

**NB Clearing out bad, fake friends** will leave you more room to strengthen your relationships with truly good, giving people – including your family. How to spot a fren-emy? Listen to how they talk about other people. If they slag off other friends to you, they are going to be doing it about you when you are not there too. Look for people with good things to say; don't be around to listen to those who don't.

## Friends' flirty fellas

One group of people that will instantly find you irresistible is the creepy partners of your girlfriends. For them, having to endure dull dinner parties with the same old couples is boring. These dos spice up the minute someone in the group – you – is single again. There's someone to flirt with, some-one to play footsie with under the dining table, someone with a bottom that can be grabbed without getting into a punch up. Or so they think. You are not the spare wheel at such parties, and you should not be treated like a serving wench from Tudor England – regardless of how much cleavage you're choosing to show that night. Keep such encounters under control by:

◆ Never being left alone with a friend's bloke.

◆ Always bringing the conversation back to your mate/his partner.

◆ Never agreeing to meet him privately.

◆ Not talking to him on the phone.

◆ Asking for a mutual friend's advice if it's getting out of control – should you tell your mate? If you do so, present the facts. Don't exaggerate or editorialise the facts. And support her, however she wants to handle it. But be prepared – he will lie and you could well be the one thrown to the dogs.

One thing I have noticed whenever I've been single is that girlfriends are very insecure – probably because of their men's behaviour. I know a lot of single girls are suddenly thrown out of the cosy-couple dinners and weekends away when they are on their own. They suddenly become forgettable and awkward. Many women don't like anything threatening around them – and as a single, sexy modern girl, you're a threat. Good friends won't exclude you, so don't worry too much about the silly ones who leave you out. Go out with your fun, secure friends who will be happy to see more of you.

## Dealing with office perverts

The other group of dodgy men who will suddenly be all over you like a rash are the office Lotharios. These dudes can sniff out a freshly single, wounded female at 50 paces – and they will hound you down, push you into the photocopying room and make inappropriate advances. You can be rude to these characters before it gets too much and one of the following happens: (a) you punch him; (b) he starts spreading rumours about you; or (c) you give in and regret it for the rest of your life. Get him off your back by pretending you have a new boyfriend who is a body builder with a black belt in karate. If his advances become totally menacing and stop you doing your work properly, go to human resources. For some reason single women are seen as fair play in the workplace. We're not.

## Coping with overbearing parents

The people in your life who will undoubtedly have more to say about your single status that anyone else are your parents. They want you to be happy and they want to have grandchildren. For these two things, they believe, you need to be in a relationship.

My mother made a really damning statement to me the other day, quite unintentionally. It was my thirty-second birthday and I was single (and happy, and living in a big city, with a great career, but …), whereas my 26-year-old brother and his wife were celebrating the birth of their first child, my adorable nephew, Archie. 'It's weird, isn't it,' my mother said, '*you* should be having our first grandchild. I always assumed it would be you. And yet, you don't even have a boyfriend!'

This was well meant but a bit sad – because it was true! I always thought it would be me too. Now my little brother has set family history: he's decided that my parents should be referred to as Granddad and Nana to their grandchildren, including any I will be lucky enough to have.

You have to remind your parents that it's not all about weddings and babies. Share with them all your successes at work, all your funny stories from nights out with the girls. Do decadent things with your mum that you couldn't do if you weren't a single working girl: take her to a spa, go away for the weekend.

However, stop sharing information with them if they use it against you. Warn them! Say, 'This is my life and I need you to support me. When I'm sad, help me. When, I'm happy, be happy for me.' If they can't be good to you, see them less. And tell them why you're removing yourself a little. They will soon learn to keep things to themselves.

Some mothers and grandmothers will start to spend a lot of time informing you of every single man who lives in their street, is related to a friend or works with them. Listen with interest – sometimes family matchmaking can work. But don't allow yourself to be bossed into dates to keep your family happy. You'll be miserable and exhausted. Just say no.

> **NB Make sure your siblings aren't unwanted conduits** of sex and dating gossip to your parents. Before you share everything, check they're not bending to your mother's nosiness at the very sniff of a home-cooked meal.

## Quick answers to single-girl put-downs

A few wise peeps will think they can laugh at your non-hooked-up-ness. Well, if you don't want them to, don't let them. You don't laugh at the guy in your department who can't spell, or the friend's husband who has a small willy (you know because she told you). Shut them up; here's how:

Jerk: 'So you're still single then?'

Modern girl: 'And you're still obnoxious/ugly/drunk.'

Jerk: 'You're single; you must be gagging for it.'

Modern girl: 'Well, at the moment I'm just gagging.'

Jerk: 'Any shags lately?'

Modern girl: 'You tell me yours first!'

Jerk: 'Can't keep hold of a man then, can you?'

Modern girl: 'Not one worth keeping hold of, no.'

Jerk: 'You should think about becoming a lesbian.'

Modern girl: 'After this conversation, I might!'

## Secrets of success

◆ Always remember your time as a single girl and how other people treated you. It will help you to see that the world is not in black and white, and that you should offer a non-judgemental kindness to everyone who crosses your path.

◆ Remember at all times that people who criticise you are often criticising themselves – through insecurity, jealousy or un-happiness. It's not about you. It's about them. Hold your head high.

◆ If someone is being unintentionally rude or hurtful, tell them. I recently said to a friend, who thought he was being light-hearted, to stop. 'I'm feeling a bit vulnerable, so if you haven't got anything 100 per cent supportive and kind to say, can you keep the jokes to yourself for a bit. I'll be back to normal soon, but at the moment, I can't take it.' He stopped and we're best friends again.

◆ Keep new romances – or your hopes of romance – to your-self, or to a select few. Others may weigh in with unwanted opinions and put-downs that will kill any future plans – or they might keep asking about a certain chap you mentioned, who hasn't called you.

◆ Being on your own, especially after leaving a traumatic relationship, can leave you feeling a little worthless and vulnerable. But don't believe it. And don't let people treat you badly. Some cruel buggers sense a weak chink in the armour, and keep pushing it. Don't let them. Don't put on a brave face, smile and then go home and cry. Walk away.

◆ As long as you can sleep soundly at night and make yourself proud, who cares what anyone else thinks about you? Self-knowledge is the most important knowledge of all.

# Chapter Five

# Curse of the exes

GROAN – THE EX FACTOR is more than an entertaining television show earning Simon Cowell his millions! Oh yes, the ex factor is something every single modern girl has to take into account when she's trying to get on with her life. While she's trying to find a man truly worthy of her, she has to deal with the ones who got away.

## Should you ever revisit romance?

Try to have some self-discipline when it comes to former lovers. We all have dreams of men changing, of suddenly coming to their senses and wanting you back – and making it work. It doesn't happen very often, although it can. We can all change. And often the shock of being dumped forces immature, crap boyfriends to become kind, commitment-keen lovers. If you want to give it a second chance, or, as we like to kid ourselves, 'just clear the air and get some answers', go for it – but don't expect him to fall at your feet and for your world to become perfect.

Sometimes going back to an ex can seem easier than striking out alone, or trying to find the same intimacy with someone new. Like the old jeans you own that have become shapeless and dirty and don't suit you any more, but you can't get rid of them, an ex is comfortable in the wrong kind of way. Get it? He's wrong for a reason. You need a new boy who fits you properly.

If you do feel it's worth giving the relationship another chance, try once. Don't keep going back and back again, repeating the same old mistakes. That won't be good for either of you. The first cut is the deepest; the second is still quite meaningful – after that it's just a blood bath of weeping, pain and mistakes.

## THE GOOD AND BAD REASONS

**Good reasons to give it another go:**

**1.** If you were just too young and you're now ready for a bit more commitment.

**2.** You got together too soon after another painful split. You treated him as your rebound thing, but now realise it meant more than that.

**3.** You allowed other people to split you up; you paid attention to others' opinions. And now you're ready to just listen to your heart.

**4.** You fell out over a stupid fight and were too proud to apologise.

**5.** Everything escalated into a drama from nothing and, before you knew it, you'd forgotten the many, many great reasons you loved each other. You needed a break. You've had one. He's the one and you're going to fight for him.

**Bad reasons to get back with an ex:**

**1.** You're bored.

**2.** You're lonely.

**3.** You're worried about being left on the shelf.

**4.** You want a baby, like yesterday, and at least you know he can get it up.

**5.** Everyone else is telling you just to put up and shut up, to take your ex back rather than ending up a childless spinster.

## How to get in touch with your exes

If you do get in touch, please, please, please don't get all The Winner Takes It All on his ass. Do not ask about his new girlfriend, or tell him you're lonely and feel like a loser. Sure, sing along with Abba at home until you lose your voice and your pillow is soaked through with tears, but if a song tells you why getting in touch with an ex is a bad idea, it's this seventies' stomper. I want to muzzle Agnetha when she's telling her ex she's lost all her self-confidence. Come on girlfriend!

Here are some healthier ways of reinstating contact:

1. Find out if he's single. If he's moved on and is with someone new, you're going to have to forget about it, or wait for that to run its natural course. If you feel you can't wait, don't keep ringing and hanging up if you hear the girlfriend's voice. Contact him once, and if he doesn't want to set a date to meet, leave it. Think about his girlfriend. This isn't her fault.

2. If you still have mutual friends, do a bit of subtle digging. Does he still miss you? Is he dating? Does he still have the same email address?

3. Don't put everything down in a letter or email. You don't know who is going to see it, or how it could be misinterpreted.

4. If you make an effort to get in touch and he ignores it, try once more – then leave it, for good! Let it go.

5. If you do have a post-split meeting, don't go to it drunk. Meet in a bar and have one glass of wine to steady your nerves, but don't have a bottle.

6. Meet somewhere mutual, such as a random bar with no memories. It's gonna be emotional enough without extra atmosphere.

7. Don't invite your mum or best friend along.

8. Try to keep the tears to a minimum, and don't go on the offensive straight away. Think carefully about what you want to say in advance. This isn't just a chance to hurl insults and then expect him to take you back. Be diplomatic.

---

**NB It's a big deal meeting up with an ex.** Don't be upset if he chickens out the day before. Likewise, if you suddenly have a change of heart or simply can't face it, cancel – and be honest. Say you fear your heart may not recover a second time but you wish him well.

---

### CLAIRE, 33

❝ You have to ask yourself why you want to get in touch with him! Now ask yourself again and be honest this time. The only reason I've ever wanted to get in touch with an ex is because I'm either (a) bored with my current relationship; or (b) there's unfinished business (such as he finished with me rather than the other way round) and I want to give him a big F*** YOU by showing up looking uber-sexy. However, a meeting with an ex invariably ends in tears – normally the next morning when you wake up next to him and nothing has changed. ❞

## When he gets in touch with you

Not all exes are created equally. But, let's face it, if you haven't chosen to rekindle any kind of relationship, steer clear. Don't be guilt-tripped into losing your mind – or heart – again with the boys below.

### The very recent ex

Too many of my friends have been sucked into the past when pleading exes have called and begged forgiveness. So they pick up the pieces, give it another go, and then go through the heartbreak all over again when the old problems start. Yes, Carrie and Mr Big had this on–off painful thang going on and it ended well, but that was scripted to give hope to 30-something women everywhere. It's not real.

Fresh splits are too raw to go back to and give another go without both of you really thinking about it seriously.

Most of the time, though, you should remember that you broke up for a reason, be it:

You'd had enough of him and his hideous ways
or
he didn't want to be with you any more.

Neither of these are good reasons to try again, are they? Hindsight should be 20/20 and you should be able to look back and think of all the things that were wrong. Write these down and remember them every time you feel yourself weakening through loneliness or fear. Put the phone down right now, modern girl! In fact, delete his number from your mobile. You're setting yourself up for a fall. Before you know it you'll go all Alanis Morissette: a screaming banshee of ex resentment.

## The distant ex

With Facebook, Friends Reunited, MySpace and the like, tracking down exes from your dim and distant past is getting really easy – and really fun. You can see what they look like now (but look at the profile photos with a pinch of salt, as they will be using their best one, and possibly quite an old one). All mine are on Facebook, so a dull hour in the office can often be spent grumbling at silly messages left by new paramours, or seeing who his new friends are. This is healthy stalking: you're safe behind your computer and he doesn't know about your mounting obsession.

If you're single, distant exes can add a boost of self-esteem and harmless flirting. The best ones are boys from school or university. You'll have had flings with them when you were still relatively young and carefree. Getting in touch with them will bring back happy memories of student days and drinking too much.

Don't expect too much if you decide to meet up in person – you've both changed a lot. A snog after a night of reminiscing could be fun, but don't automatically believe you can pick up where you left off. See how it goes, of course, enjoy going 'high school' for a bit and see where it takes you. This is just the kind of harmless flirting you need when you're newly single.

**NB Remember, you haven't just grown up in the decade** since you last saw your ex. You look different too and so does he – and seeing him could ruin all your what-could-have-been fantasies. I recently met up with the university love of my life for drinks. It was ten years since we'd seen each other – and I'd like to think I looked better (what with the blue eye shadow and rugby shirts being consigned to the dustbin) – but as for him?! Well, he was overweight, balding and had a sweat problem. I had mixed feelings about the night: I got to show him how fabulous I was and what he'd missed (he dumped me horribly by kissing someone else in front of me) but now I can only picture the current Mr Ex, not the old one who inspired my crush on Michael Vartan. Such a shame.

## The romantic ex

Not all exes are created equally. Some will just call you up drunk and say sorry and expect it all to be OK. Others really push the boat out to woo you back. These guys have more promise in the long term. They know how wonderful you are and how lucky they would be to gain your trust again. If your ex does at least three of the following, you should meet him somewhere neutral for a coffee to discuss your feelings:

♦ He makes you a CD with songs that actually mean something.

♦ He writes you a beautiful poem, or buys you a book of poetry and inscribes it with a heartfelt message.

- He flies to wherever you are in the world and begs you to listen to him.

- He sends you a beautiful piece of jewellery so perfect you could have chosen it yourself.

- He writes a letter acknowledging every mistake he's made, why he knows it was wrong and how he's going to improve.

- He offers to hold your heart forever, promises not to break it, and gives in on a massive hurdle you had together – be it religion, children, marriage or his parents, and so on.

## The stalker ex

This one just won't take no for an answer. If he wasn't unattractive enough when you dumped him, this is just making it worse. Don't delete this guy's number from your phone: you need to recognise it so that you know not to answer it when he calls. And calls. And calls. Put your phone on silent when you're on a date or asleep so that he can't disturb you.

Don't give in to his demands to see you. You need to rip the plaster off in one go. Every time you afford him an audience he'll get fresh hope and think perhaps you feel the same, even if you're telling him no. If he needs to get stuff off his chest, let him do it in an email. Meeting stalker exes – even exes you no longer have feelings for – will be emotionally draining and difficult. You won't get anything good out of it; this ex type won't even make you feel wanted and sexy. You'll come away feeling like a heartless bitch or a lucky escapee. Don't let this dude's pleading soften your will.

## They always want you back

All of the above ex types – even the men who treated you badly and dumped you – will want you back at some point, laydeez. Men are either too stupid to realise you've fallen out of love and are working out how to dump them, or they're too cocky to realise what a great prize they have in you and think that being single again will be fun.

In general, I've found through my own experiences and those of friends and family, that women are astutely mourning the demise of a relationship while they are still in it. Us girls tend to spend anything from six months to five years asking questions of themselves and their partner, asking to go to relationship therapy or wanting to spend more time together, whereas the men selfishly go on in their own sweet way, not worrying that you're crying yourself to sleep every night or wondering why you're spending more and more time away from home.

Suddenly, when the bed is cold, the fridge is empty and there's no one to take his side in an argument, he thinks of you. And thinks how much you supported him, loved him, fed him, carried him, paid for him, worshipped him, organised him ... But you are under no obligation to take him back – even if he's saying all the things you wanted to hear when you were still together. And you'll be amazed at how strong you can be, I promise you. Time and distance make you see his flaws in bright sunlight, and you'll be able to say (and mean it), 'I don't want you back.'

## No regrets

As long as you did the following before the split, I promise you you'll have no regrets:

- You talked to him.

- You offered to listen to the issues he had with you.

- You asked how you could change the key things he didn't like.

- You put the idea of therapy out there – together or individually.

- You cried your heart out, he saw you, and didn't do anything.

- You asked him to be kind to you, and he couldn't show you kindness.

## When the parents get involved

Keep them out of it! This is why you shouldn't tell parents or siblings too much during your relationship or when it's finished. It'll make getting back together or even moving on so much more difficult. My parents still check in every now and again to make sure I haven't had a change of heart regarding my ex-husband and ex-boyfriend and it's annoying. It just reminds me of the past. I know it's because they care and they just want better for me, but I wish they'd shsh! and move on like I have.

It's worse when the ex's family gets involved. My ex-boyfriend's mother continued writing to me, telling me how tough our split was on her. Be polite (resentment should not be placed at anyone's feet by the two people in the relationship), but don't feel you have to stay in touch. You need to cope on your own, and look after yourself. Kindly and gently stop contact if you can't stay in touch and recover.

## Why are exes so comforting?

They're familiar and you know how they work. Better the devil you know? Well, there's a lot to be said for that – but if he's a devil, you deserve better! You may not want to sleep with someone new, to teach a new man about your wobbly bits and G spot, but you're going to have to – and it will be worth it. Just keep remembering how knee-trembling it is to have that first kiss, or that first shag, with someone new. Don't go for comfort with an ex when you can have passion with no baggage with someone you haven't even given a try yet.

---

### DANIELLE, 34

❝ An ex is only so comforting because this is someone you were once very special to. They give you the hope that someone once found you attractive and funny enough to spend time with you – so you can't be all that bad! In extreme emergency situations (if you're still on talking terms), the ex can tell you where you are going wrong with new men, although the heartbreaking truth is that they are also a reminder of someone who you might think is great, but who doesn't want to be with you. If you have close boyfriends, rely on them for romance advice instead. Sex makes everything messy. ❞

## Keeping new–old romances quiet

If you do decide to give it another go with an ex, think about keeping it quiet for a while. People will be quick to judge – in a good way! They care about you, and they saw how confused/angry/exhausted/heartbroken you were before. They want to shake you and scream 'DON'T GO THERE!' But you know what? No one knows what really happens in a relationship, or understands the chemistry between two people except the couple themselves. If you don't want those around you to get nosey, interfere or give you unwanted opinions, keep your hook-up between the two of you. At least until you know if it's going to go anywhere, or that it's a mistake.

If you are going to give it another go, get the old issues out there immediately – and then listen to his issues too. Both of you need to agree to change and work at it, and to leave baggage at the door. Don't just repeat old patterns. If there's too much resentment (often caused by past neglect or new fears), you haven't got a fighting chance.

## Sex with an ex – yes or no?

It's there on tap, he knows what you look like naked, and it's so comfortable you can get your orgasm without too many theatrics. You've seen his 'O' face so it won't spoil the moment. Sounds great, huh? Er, no!

A good few months after I had split up with my ex-boyfriend, I had only cried twice. Both times were after we met up to swap things or to talk about things – and ended up in bed. The few hours of comfortable collapse are not worth the next few days of confusion and regrets and disappointment with yourself.

Sex complicated everything. We didn't even have a highly sexual, passionate relationship (we started off as friends and companionship definitely set the scene for our romance) but the ex-sex was so easy that I started reading things into it. He did love me more than I thought; he was the best man I was ever going to get. Listen to Jermaine Stewart: where exes are concerned, it's definitely better not to take your clothes off if you want to have a good time (AKA a good life!)

---

**NB If you truly feel there's enough distance** between the split and the offered shag, and you're healthy about the whole thing – and horny – try it once. Afterwards, if you find yourself thinking too much about it, or hoping he'll call you, you're not over him. Stop. He is an itch that shouldn't be scratched. Sadly, you can't build a long-lasting, devoted relationship on being good between the sheets alone.

---

# Secrets of success

◆ Beware of false attachment. It's not the man you still love, its coupledom. Even in the dark times of being a single girl you should remember why you split up and not rose-tint your past relationships.

◆ Saying no to an ex who wants you back will break your heart. You will remember the good times, and be flattered by his apologies and musings on your past love, and your heart will stop when you see his email or hear his voice on your phone. That's natural. That doesn't mean you have to take him back.

◆ If they do get in touch, and you talk, don't lie about anything – particularly about having a new boyfriend if you haven't got one. This just makes you look needy and seems to imply you feel you need to be in a relationship to be important. It's actually more powerful to say you're single and loving it!

◆ Try to be realistic about an ex getting in touch: the reasons are probably not so flattering (he wants sex, he's lonely or he can't find anyone else).

◆ The only reason to have sex with an ex is if he was really bad in bed, and you know reminding yourself of this will stop you thinking about him forever. But then again, why bother? And if he's improved in the sack you'll just feel bad that you trained him up for his next victim.

◆ The positive is, once you get into the flow of being single and moving to your own rhythm, 99 per cent of the time you won't want your annoying ex back. It really is too late to apologise for a lot of strong, modern girls out there. You'll be surprised how easily you'll be able to say, 'Thanks but no thanks.'

# Chapter Six

# Dating rules
# for the single girl

ETTING A DATE, FINDING A MATE, before it's too late – it's hell out there! A date is never just a date: your self-esteem and future dreams are all wrapped up in the pressure of one night out with a new man. But how do you navigate this – while appearing normal – to get what you want? Read on, girlfriends.

## How to meet fabulous single men

God, if I knew how to meet all the best single men, I'd be married to George Clooney and living in a mansion on Lake Como by now, my man-trapping ability would be so top-notch. However, here are some things I do know:

◆ You won't meet someone if you are hiding away from the world. As comfy as your couch is, and as protected as you feel staying in with your DVD player, you have to get out there. Take as much time as you need bolstering yourself up and recovering from heartbreak and disappointment, but when you know you're ready to find love, get out.

◆ When you go out looking for love, treat it as if you are going out for a love-ly night and to talk to love-ly men. The slightest whiff of desperation or entrapment and even the nicest guy will run for the nearest exit (even if it's the window of an apartment on the thirtieth floor).

◆ See it how it is: a night out that holds a lot of potential. Dress up – play up your pluses and hide or deny your weak spots. Confidence is sexy. So is a warm smile. These will be your two biggest weapons when you're out on the pull.

◆ The best thing to do is be yourself – your most wonderful self – at all times, outside your own home, or during family time at your parents. You never know when a thunderbolt will hit, for you or your next boyfriend. If you're single and not happy about it, hide it. Be fabulous, not needy; reflective, not lonely; fun, not paranoid. It sounds difficult, but I promise you that with the right frame of mind, friends and makeup bag, you'll do it.

## Traditional places to find men

Try looking for men at any kind of sporting event, except football, perhaps, where they are usually moaning, swearing and generally not into flirting, such is their love and attention devoted to the beautiful game. Wrestling and boxing matches are great. They're about 99 per cent men, and the atmosphere is sexy and daring, and you can play the lost-little-woman thing men adore. It can also work acting confused at a rugby game, which shouldn't be too hard, seeing as it is, well, confusing.

Hotel bars are perfect. So many people are travelling on their own it's easy to strike up friendly banter over the mixed nuts and a gin and tonic. Hopefully, just the fact that they are there (think Ritz Carltons not Travel Taverns) means they are well-travelled go-getters with a good future. You can also be a little braver and stay out a little later, knowing your bedroom and escape is only a short lift ride away. Don't give him your hotel room number or surname, just in case you go off him before he goes off you. And although the promise of sex is a tempting one, seeing as the aforementioned hotel bedroom is only a few steps away, keep in mind he is essentially a stranger at this point – and this probably will turn out to be a one-night stand/brief holiday fling.

## What about the office?

The office is still the number-one place for women (who haven't already found their beloved at school or university) to hook up. Well, you spend most of your conscious life between those drab walls, so who can blame you for looking to liven the workplace up a bit.

If you've got your eye on someone, spend a bit more time working late if he does (even if you're just downloading photos onto Facebook), in the hope of a coffee conversation. Start going to his favoured lunch spot (no, I'm not advising stalking, just a little light detective work). If he eats in the staff canteen, cope with it. If he's signed up to some work-related club or society, join it. Accept invites out with your colleagues for drinks after work. If he's as great as you think, he'll be invited too. Look for a work-related reason to email him, and follow up with a 'can you explain more over a cup of tea' manoeuvre. If all else fails, the office Christmas party is a great place for water-cooler romances to heat up. Just don't get too drunk and ridiculous, or he'll think it's just that: a bit of drunk-and-ridiculous flirting with no long-term substance.

---

**NB Until he is yours,** limit the amount of people you talk to about him – just your most trusted friend within the office, and not even her if you know she's the office gossip. Keep it outside if you can. It can backfire either way. If you get together, she'll feel she has the right to drone on with unwanted advice, and perhaps even share it with him. If you don't get together with him, she'll feel the need to nudge you in the ribs or give you a pitying glance every time he saunters to the photocopier.

## When you're travelling

A surprising amount of people I know have met their partners on a plane or at an airport. So when you're single, dress up a bit when you're in transit. I'm not talking leopard skin and a full face of makeup, but do make sure you're clean, wearing flattering clothes (I'm always tempted to fly bare-faced, in a duvet-size tracksuit and Uggs – and regret it the minute a gorgeous guy boards). If you're not lucky enough to have some hunk sitting next to you, get into the same bathroom-break rhythm, or chat to him at the luggage carousel. The chance is you're both somewhere new for a few days – and new friends could be handy.

## Get your friends to help you

Meeting a man in a bar is the most obvious one: why else do singles hit them, come hell or high water three nights a week, if they're not hoping cupid will spike their drink? The best thing is to go with one partnered-up pal whose sole mission is to get you sorted. You don't need any competition. She'll be your eyes and ears, and then your publicist when an interested male approaches (and you won't worry that she'll run off with him). I've recently heard from a few male friends that they pay compliments to the friend of the girl they fancy to (a) show they are an all-round good guy; and (b) to keep her happy, so that she'll stay out with you for a little while longer. So don't get annoyed if he says he loves her dress. Trust your gut instinct. She may be getting all the flattering remarks, but are you getting the eye contact and sly smiles?

Through friends is the easiest option. You get the background check first, so you know, most importantly, if he's single and looking for a decent woman to have some fun with (that is, you). Don't work through everyone's friends like a tornado, however. Limit yourself. And don't share too much sex info if it does develop; they don't want to know, even if they think they do. Until you hook up, you can plough your mates for info about him, especially demanding any comments he has made about you – however flippant ('Zoe was telling me she loves Italy,' and even those little comments that show you've registered with him). Accept invites to friends' parties, dinners and theatre trips; anything where you'll get to meet available men – or women who can introduce you to their available men.

### SARAH, 32

❝ I'd been single for a few months and, although I was still recovering from a bad split, it was summer and I fancied a little bit of love action. Wonderfully – but rather tragically – I was living in a city where 99 per cent of the men – and indeed my close friends – were gay. This wasn't helping, so I had a night out with two fellow single girls. We went to one dull bar, followed by another stuffy bar ... then stumbled across a fabulous place with amazing cocktails, a good vibe and lots of handsome men. A Barry Manilow medley came on, and I had to text my diva pal Robert, a huge Fanilow! He replied simply: "REMOVE YOURSELF FROM THAT GAY BAR NOW. THEY WON'T HAVE YOUR BABIES." Oops! ❞

### NEW WAYS TO FIND MEN TO DATE

- Public transport. Everyone is bored and looking for anything to amuse them. If you stick to the same commuting time, you'll get to notice the same faces – particularly the handsome ones. Break the ice by talking about the weather, delays or what's in the day's news (if he's reading a paper).

- Poke someone dishy on Facebook 'accidentally', then start a conversation. Trawl through friends of friends, and ask friends if any potential ones are single.

- Go to male-dominated evening classes. Try plumbing, brickwork or DIY for beginners. You could find a man and some handy skills!

- Join film or book clubs. Sensitive guys like these things as much as the ladies. Just don't expect to read too much Jane Austen or Sophie Kinsella!

## Making the right first impression

People make up their minds about you in the first few seconds of meeting you: your clothes, voice, body, face, that certain *je ne sais quoi*. This makes those first seconds crucial. A bad move here could set you back hours, if not forever.

I have a naturally grumpy face, which, combined with my height – I'm nearly 1.8m (6ft) – leads those who don't know me to think I'm a bit of a bitch. As soon as my friends told me this, I could work on looking less intimidating and more approachable. How many men had I put off in the past with my totally misleading stern demeanour? Thankfully, with my friends' honesty I learned to smile more and be less rigid with body contact. Ask your friends what kind of first impression you might be making. Some offputting things that are easy to change include:

◆ A high-pitched squeaky voice.

◆ A strange, loud laugh.

◆ Not looking people in the eye.

◆ Smirking.

◆ Playing, tugging or picking at any part of your anatomy or clothing.

◆ Dirty or stained clothes.

◆ Holes in anything.

◆ Lipstick on your teeth, or food in your teeth.

◆ Unleashed underwear – a fallen bra strap here, an exposed thong there.

◆ A face like thunder and pulsating veins.

## Conversation starters

We'll discuss how to look dateable and sexy in Chapter 8, but for now, once you've trapped him with your eye candy, how do you keep him there with your personality; that is, what words can come out of your mouth that will make him ask you out for a date?

Well, all men are different, of course, so I'll try to limit the sweeping generalisations. The first thing to remember is that even the most handsome, charismatic men can be insecure and nervous. Put the boot on the other foot: you may have an I'm-woman-hear-me-roar exterior on a night out looking for dreamboats, but inside you're lacking in confidence and thinking, 'Why would anyone want me?' Men are the same. They often just hide it better by being insensitive jerks.

So, if someone catches your eye, break the ice with a smile (one that reaches the eyes, no shifty darting gazes, please) and a compliment: 'I love that tie' is simple and not too personal (if he's wearing one, of course. If not, transfer the nice comment to another piece of attire).

If that seems too bold, you can always just sidle up to where he's standing and ask for directions to the restaurant, the car park or the loos. Or, if he's at the bar, nestle in and ask him if he's been served yet. Chit-chat about your shared environment does not force you to put yourself out there too much if you're nervous. So once you've got near to him, chat about the scene or the music, and laugh at some fellow guests who have drunk too much or don't seem to have many dancing skills. If there's food or fancy cocktails, bond by making him seem intelligent or manly by asking for his guidance and suggestions – most men love this, even if they don't love you (yet!).

Always check out the news or a few fun blog sites before you leave for a manhunt – random facts will pop into your head when you're stumbling for some first words, so at least if you're well briefed on popular culture your conversation will be current and interesting.

## Get yourself a wingman

If you have a friend who is your fall guy, your second at Thunder Road, do get her to come out on dates with you to take the pressure off. Just make sure you choose the right girl:

◆ She should be in a happy, committed relationship. You cannot squabble over men; bitch fights are ugly and put every kind of man off – except possibly drunk banker wankers!

◆ She should want the very best for you. She's not a bitch. She genuinely wants you to meet a great guy and be happy.

◆ She should know you inside and out, and know your type of man. This allows her to be your eyes and ears when you're too busy downing your Pinot Noir or nervously checking your appearance in your hand mirror.

◆ She should be able to read your body language, and you should both work in sync. An eyebrow lift will be all that's needed for her to know to clear off. Plan a few signals that can help you out of a bad spot, or into a good one.

◆ She should be a good reflection on you; that is, the man in your gaze should think, 'She's cool, and her mate's cool – she must be nice and normal!'

**KATIE, 28**

❛ My mate Sara had been single for ages and it was painful to watch. She was pretty, lovely, a real catch – and yet she'd stay in moping and feeling unlovable. We work together, and I would see her every day and feel so bad for her. So, every night for one week, I dragged her off to various man hot spots around the city. I knew the good and bad bits of her ex, which celebs she fancied and what she needed, so although that week didn't produce her next one-and-only, it got her back into the game. I got her talking to lots of suitable men and opened up her eyes to being dateable again! ❜

## Smirting

It's bad, bad, bad, but you can try 'smirting' – an old favourite of mine. Ask the man you desire for a cigarette or a light. So you smoke yourself into a flirting position. Now, with smoking bans, this has the added bonus of getting you away from the crowd and outside into the peace and quiet. Smokers are so aware of their nasty habit that smirting is a triple treat: it's a great small-talk starter, it gets you alone and is an instant bond (you can indulge your dirty little secret together).

## First dates

Those first dates are always awkward and scary – so don't worry. We all feel the same, men and women alike! Don't wind yourself up by asking your friends for first-date horror stories. We all have them, and bad tales won't keep you focused. When going into a first-date scenario, be careful to keep your feet on the ground. Don't expect magic. Expect him to be wearing one thing you think is naff, to say one thing you think is a bit stupid; you're strangers dancing around potential sex – you're going to be overly critical and judgemental. Why don't you turn journalist at the beginning of the date, to put him at ease and to learn things about him that you could have in common? So, yes, interview him. Not aggressively à la Jeremy Paxman, but softly, softly in an *OK!* magazine way: where did he grow up, does he have siblings, what country does he want to visit next? And so on.

If your conversation becomes a little slow, don't feel it would be vain to give him an abridged version of your CV. It fills a gap in the conversation, and will give you a chance to big yourself up – for his benefit and yours.

All you can expect from a first date is to know if you want a second date. And, whatever your mental outcome, I hope he feels the same way – as unrequited second dates are painful for either sex. Good signs that another date is on the cards are: you both laugh a lot; the hours fly by; and you don't want the night to end – that is, you'd quite like to have your wicked way with him – and you're pretty sure he feels the same way. Sadly, as we'll discuss further in the next chapter, this is not advisable.

When it comes to one-night stands, double standards still exist – even safe, non-drunk, passionate ones. You do hear about one-night stands ending in marriages, but more often you hear of them ending with a disappointed girl jumping every time her phone rings. And it isn't him – the boy who got her to open up on the first date. She feels like she's been punched in the stomach, and it hurts. If the passion is there, hold on to that sentiment until the next date, when more of a personal relationship has been forged through a few days of emails and phone calls. But good going, girl. Passion is a biggie!

## Second dates

When you go out the second time you could offer to sort out what you do together, to take the pressure off him, and offer to pay at the end too, if he paid last time – but accept graciously if he insists that it's his treat again. You can be more open on a second date. If he's back for seconds, he must have had a taster of something that he wants more of. Feel free to get a little tipsier, flirty, touchy, feely – this will make you all the more adorable. Do not, however, go deeply into your troubled childhood, bad past relationships or ticking clock. Save this for when you're boyfriend and girlfriend, and he can't run away so easily.

## How to rock your body

It's not all about how you look and what you say, it's about chemistry and general all-round yumminess. The quickest and easiest way to get this is through using the right body language:

1. Hold a gaze for a few seconds, then look away shyly. Don't gawp or stare at his crotch during the whole date.

2. Suggestively tug on your blouse, subtly and naturally.

3. Stroke your own neck, as above.

4. Twiddle your hair between your fingers alluringly.

5. Lean in to him when he talks.

6. Cross and uncross your legs when sat down – think Sharon Stone (with knickers on!).

7. Touch his arm lightly when he makes a joke or seems nervous.

8. Keep your knees facing him to show interest.

9. Don't fold your arms or lean back – it shows defensiveness.

10. Be natural: if you want to give him a jokey punch, or – God forbid – sit on his knee, do it. Just be aware of any special issues he has!

## Blind dates

Generally, blind dates are considered a bad idea, because, as we all know, it's not about how someone is on paper, it's all about chemistry: pheromones. It's those darn things that mix and mingle, fill the air with that special tingle. If time, desperation or pressures have led you down the blind-date path, make sure you have your emergency exits covered.

Before you even accept this romantic invitation, do your research. Grill your friendly fixers. Get on the Web. Google his company and hometown. See if he's on any blog sites. It's worryingly easy to find out info these days. If you're alerted by anything dodgy, cancel. Don't worry about it – you've never seen him, so you're not going to have to worry about bumping into him. If you push ahead, plan some escape routes: get a friend to call a few hours into the evening to check you're enjoying yourself and to throw a fake wobbly if you need to run away. Plan a code word in advance. 'Moobs' works.

You can also pre-plan an early departure by warning him you have a 7.00 am meeting or personal-training session, or that you still have a file to read before work tomorrow. Then, of course, if he's wonderful and the old pheromones are racing, he'll get extra flattered when you 'cancel' your meeting or trainer, or yell, 'Sod the report!' while delicately stroking your collar bone and giggling at all his jokes.

## When do you go from dating to serious mating?

There are three key signs that your relationship has hit a more serious note; watch out for these:

1. He introduces you as his girlfriend. To anyone. Even to the man he buys his beers from on the street corner.

2. His friends and/or family have met you and are making an effort – or resent you fiercely for stealing their boy away. Either extreme reaction shows it's serious.

3. He gives up a boys' night to stay in with you when you've had a rough day.

There are other more obvious things, of course: he wants to know what you'd call your children, he asks you to move in, he proposes marriage, but these three hints I've outlined appear much sooner and come as a great insight into whether he's commitment-ready.

**NB Lots of modern girls multi-date.** This has definite pros and cons. On the plus side, you've always got some man interest. Even when one flirtation fizzles out – as so many sadly do – there's someone at the end of an email to make you feel sexy again, suggesting he takes you out and treats you. On the negative side, if you're dating all these different fellas, when do you get the chance to shave your legs or see your mates (not necessarily in that order)? And it's very rare that everything is equal. You will normally like one man more than the others. If this is the case, just multi-date for as long as you feel comfortable, and certainly don't multi-shag. That's just dirty. By the way, if you are multi-dating, you might want to be dating old-fashioned gentlemen who believe in paying for ladies – otherwise this scheme could get very expensive.

## Bad dates

Don't be too hard on yourself. Sure, blame should be split 50/50 – unless he brings his mum on dates and burps at the table! If it just isn't working, you can't force it. Don't let it put you off dating in general, but learn from it instead. Were you so nervous you couldn't talk properly? How can you improve? Did you get too drunk? Stay sober next time. Did you share too much? Learn when to shut up for next time. Think back to his facial expressions and answers – you'll learn about yourself as a date. And as we all know, knowledge is power.

## Keep-a-man business plan

Once you've seen someone you like, and arranged a date, the work really begins. Follow this business model to success:

### Finances

Know your worth, girlfriend! Don't sell yourself short. If he's rude, dismissive, uninterested, selfish, and so on, he's not for you. Value yourself higher. If he's showing these low-rent characteristics on the first date, he'll only get worse. Before you re-embark on serious dating, get your friends and family to tell you a few reasons why you're worth a million bucks!

### Advertising

Put it out there, sister. Show him what you've got. When first impressions are worth so much, sometimes it is important to invest in good looks and exteriors. Imagine you're a billboard – what do you want to sell and who are you trying to attract? You want to sell yourself to the best, highest-paying consumer of great girls, right? Look your best.

### Marketing

Once you've got him on a date, it's stage two of selling. These are the more subtle ways of drawing your dream man in: highlighting some of your advantages (a nice flat, conversational Italian, a penchant for silky underwear), while hiding some of the less attractive aspects on offer (mad parents and a collection of china dolls). If you're unsure what falls into what category, ask an honest male friend. When I first moved into my new flat as a single girl, my good friend

Rob told me straight, 'Hide that oversized teddy bear that your ex bought you. Or even better, bin it!'

### Return on investment

Very quickly, by date two or three, you will be able to tell if this guy has got everything you need – not forever, but just to make you happy and let you think about making it serious. If you get the slightest feeling of nausea or danger, cut your losses and run. Trust your instincts. Don't allow something small like dirty shoes to put you off, but something bigger, like an overwhelming desire to visit grave sites at night, should set you on the right path to yay or nay.

## *Secrets of success*

◆ How to meet men? Smile – all the time. They'll come to you. They might not be the ones you want, but practise looking friendlier and enjoy the nice attention.

◆ DUI (dialling under the influence) – it's evil and should be illegal! When you get a new, hot guy's digits, don't put them into your phone for a while. Leave it for him to call you. And certainly don't drink and dial. You can't win – you'll either look desperate, like a silly drunk, or he'll say come over and you'll have dodgy sex – without even getting a free dinner first!

◆ If your prowling partner lets you down and disappears off with the guy you've got your eye on, don't trust her again. Get a new wingman.

◆ If you and your single pal are each other's wingmen, set some ground rules. A good one my friend has just installed is fair and stops fights: if you both quite like the same guy, and meet him the same night, let him decide. If you spotted him two seconds before your friend (because you walked in the bar first, basically), those two seconds do not make him your property. If you have been chasing him for weeks and your friend sees him later, that's different. She should keep her hands off.

◆ It's not worth losing girlfriends for boys – unless a girl really shows an evil side, or the man is a David Beckham lookalike, who treats you like gold and proposes. Your girlfriends are probably going to be around longer than the majority of these dates, so treat them with the respect they deserve.

◆ Who pays on dates? Offer to pay half, offer twice; on the third time say thanks – and then try to contribute somehow   – pay for the taxi, a nightcap or the cinema tickets on the third or fourth date.

# Chapter Seven

# Sex and the single girl

G ETTING IT ON IS ONE of life's greatest pleasures – and it's free! Well, almost. Sadly, shagging the wrong person, or shagging at the wrong time, can cost you dearly; Mother Nature's greatest freebie has a way of going wrong and biting you on your behind. As George Michael sang so eloquently, 'sex is natural – sex is good'. Yes indeed, sex is something that we *should do* – just carefully!

## What to do when you're not getting any

If you're not getting any sex, forget cold showers, forget running away to join a nunnery. Instead, gather a memory bank of your best sex memories or trawl through your most satisfying fantasies – and learn a bit of 'DIY'; be it by your own hand, a vibrating rabbit/dolphin/tongue/cock-a-like or a shower-head with warm water gushing out of it. Don't go to prostitutes. Don't damage yourself with a shampoo bottle. Don't feel guilty and deprive yourself of pleasure because you think it's dirty, nasty or against your religion. Oh come on, the chemicals released with an orgasm will keep your hormones in check and your moods on an even keel until you find someone to do it with.

---

**JEN, 31**

❝ When I'm not getting any sex I tend to feel very sorry for myself. It's an animalistic sadness and need that becomes obsessional – even if life is good in every other area. Sometimes when I want the sex without the boyfriend, I go off on holiday with a few close girlfriends and have protected no-strings-attached sex with a stranger who I won't run the

➡

> risk of seeing again. I spot someone I fancy, and then spend a few days getting to know him. He can woo me, but I know I'm going to sleep with him so it's unnecessary really! 🙶

## Too much satisfaction?

I know quite a few young ladies, who will remain nameless, who have become far too attached to their battery-operated equipment. Calm down, girls – you don't want to rub your clitoris away! When you're getting through three packets of batteries in a month, it's time to get out more. Sure, you and your plastic pal can enjoy an occasional Sunday *à deux*. But when you're turning down dates, or not going to the gym because you'd rather stay in and masturbate, you've got a problem. Your body can become too used to certain techniques too, so don't just do the same thing. Remember, a real cock is best because:

1. It's warm.

2. It has a man attached, which is useful for kissing and for talking dirty with. And he can make you a cup of tea afterwards.

> **NB When you do start dating,** don't introduce the sex toys too soon. Men find them intimidating until they feel secure with their lady. Sure, a kinky one-night stand and a bag of tricks is one thing, but if you like the guy, play it cool and enjoy his body. How nice to have another person in bed with you at last!

## Getting back in the saddle

Going through a bad split can really leave your self-worth in the gutter. Believe me, I know. Mentally revealing yourself – physically and emotionally – can be tough, a bit of an ordeal, so make sure you're ready. Don't push yourself into anything too quickly. I've always left a couple of months between an old lover and newcomer. It stops your head getting too messy. If you do jump into the sack, don't beat yourself up about it – something made you want to do it and you should always trust your gut instincts. Move on and think about what you've learned from the experience. Did you enjoy it? What was better/worse than what you'd been used to? What do you wish you'd tried?

## How to handle getting naked in front of a stranger

My last ex, towards the end of our relationship, started twittering on about me being a chubster. Fab, thanks! I'll take that into my next relationship, shall I, and sleep in a wet suit so the poor unsuspecting bloke doesn't have to see my old, fat flesh! When we first split, his words ricocheted around my head and I started to think, 'Why would anyone else ever find me attractive or, God forbid, want to see me naked?' I started judging myself and thinking I wasn't good enough.

Thankfully, escaping his nastiness and regrouping (and doing yoga), after only a few months away from him I realised that (a) he was a twat; and (b) we always judge ourselves more harshly than anyone else does – especially normal men. Yes, they look at Page Three Girls and the

Pussycat Dolls, but they know these bimbettes aren't real (and secretly find them a bit scary/intimidating/stupid).

Men are not looking at your cellulite or muffin tops. In fact, when you do go to bed with someone, he's got his own issues – the main one being is he going to give you an orgasm (quite right too!).

Think about it: when you've been flirting, dating, gagging for some bloke for a while and you finally make it under the duvet, are you thinking, 'His dick should be a bit bigger' or 'He's too hairy'? No, you're too busy thinking about yourself and your own performance – and then finally, I hope you're thinking, 'Yum, yum, this is fantastic!'

If you know there's a good chance you'll be shagging a new man on a particular night, prepare yourself – this will really give your self-confidence a boost:

◆ Wax, tweeze and shave yourself into oblivion.

◆ Fake tan yourself, but far enough in advance not to leave orange streaks on his sheets.

◆ Treat yourself to some new sexy underwear. Red or sheer never miss.

◆ When a relationship shows hook-up potential, get your ass up the gym.

◆ If things really are desperate, go for those instant-inch wrap treatments the day of your date.

◆ Diminish your tummy by avoiding salt, fizzy drinks and chewing gum on the big day.

◆ Nice hands and feet are a treat – get a manicure and pedicure.

◆ Lash extensions are my new secret weapon. They are quite pricey but last for up to two months, and give you come-to-bed eyes in the evening, and instantly gorgeous eyes in the morning when you wake up (and with them on, you don't need to wear any other eye makeup so you avoid the really rough Gothic look when you've got a sweaty sex face).

♦ If you're planning a seduction at your place, stock up on candles. They are wonderfully forgiving and sexy all at once. Everyone looks good when lit by a flickering flame.

---

### ABIGAIL, 38

❝ How do I handle flashing my bits for the first time in front of a new man? It's simple: I make sure the lights are turned out. I figure this is better than my insecure action of my twenties, when I got totally drunk so that I lost all my inhibitions. But at any age, it's good to remember that by the time you're in bed most men are just so grateful to have a real, keen and warm girl in bed with them that they don't care about any extra lumps and bumps. ❞

---

## Sleeping with the enemy

If by any chance you've slept with a jerk who feels he can pass comment on your less-than-perfect posterior, take action. Leave and get dressed with dignity. Never contact him again. Process his criticism. If it makes sense, work on it – improve yourself and focus on the positives. You'll soon be feeling fabulous; while, I can promise you, a loser like that will spend his days masturbating alone or shagging very unhappy women.

## The morning after the night before

It's gonna be awkward the next morning. Take that for granted. Sex adds a strange dynamic to any relationship, however well you know someone. Make post-shag time as simple as possible by following a few simple instructions:

**When you've got it on at his place:** if you're in any position to think ahead after the deed is done, regroup and put your underwear back on, go to the bathroom to check your hair/ makeup/love bites – and if you pick up any weird vibes at all (sudden grumpiness/rudeness/over-lovingness (such as talk about marriage or babies) get yourself out of there double-quick (pretend that you have an early meeting or personal-trainer appointment that you can't miss at 7.00 am).

**When you've got it on at your place:** offer him the use of your shower/towels, keep a new spare toothbrush, bring him a glass of water but don't go over the top and make him a midnight feast (unless you're both starving and bond in the kitchen together), set your alarm and say you won't be offended if he can't stay but that he's more than welcome to. If he does leave, it doesn't mean he doesn't like you. We all work hard and have early starts, so we need our sleep. Do be offended only if it's a Saturday night.

## Second-time sex

I think that getting it on in the morning is often better than the first time, when you're a bit drunk or nervous. Yes, the sun's come up so it's a bit brighter and lighter – and your breath isn't so hot, but don't automatically shy away from it. Keep the curtains drawn, stay under the sheets and know that his breath is just as bad as yours. If the sex is good the morning after, you're on to a winner. Enjoy it!

## Can you have good one-night-stand sex?

Of course, sex can be good if it's just for the one night. Otherwise we wouldn't keep putting ourselves out there, would we? Just be aware that it could just be that: a one-night one-off. The negative of that is that he's probably not the guy you're going to marry – so don't hit the sack if you want to show him you're more of a long-term option. The positive of that is that you really let your hair down and go wild, live out fantasies and make sure he satisfies you first. You really don't need to be concerned with him. A one-night stand is all about you.

## The real STDs

As sensible modern girls, I'm assuming you're all being healthy and sensible when it comes to shagging and are always using protection. I've started keeping a condom in my wallet (the same one has been in there a depressingly long time, I must say, but it's better to be safe than sorry). However, if you do notice anything strange about your sexual health, get yourself to your doctor or hospital sexual health (GUM) clinic. Things that just aren't right include: strange smelling or coloured discharge, itching, lumps or bleeding. Don't worry too much, just take precautions and follow up anything unusual.

Emotionally, the sexually transmitted diseases that have affected me and my friend more recently are those of the heart. It seems that as soon as you go to bed with someone you vaguely like, you catch a number of nasty afflictions:

◆ **Confusion.** Is it love or lust? Our heart says one thing; our head says another. Who knows? We'll have to shag him again to find out.

◆ **Amnesia.** If he's good in the sack, all other flaws are forgotten. He doesn't call, he hasn't got any friends, and he's cheap. Who cares? He makes you come.

◆ **Schizophrenia.** One minute you're enjoying the wildest high, and then you suffer a debilitating low. Shagging releases feel-good feelings, then when you're on your own after he leaves the hangover sets in. You might be forced to ride the post-shag roller coaster until he calls – or until a week passes and he hasn't called, and you then get off the ride and head to the House of Horror.

## Amazing sex

An incredible fact has just been uncovered by scientists studying how human behaviour differs around the world. Research was made in small tribes, big cities and everywhere in between and it was noted that human beings – regardless of colour, class, or nationality – love three things more than anything else: eating, shitting and shagging. Basically, we're the same as animals. And all humans are driven by the same needs and pleasures. Think about it, we're obsessed with all three.

Of these three, the only one that requires another person is shagging. Eating and shitting is perfectly acceptable on your own. So when you need someone else to do it, how can you make sex amazing?

1. **Know your body.** Look at it, feel it, work your way around it. Listen to what gets you panting, and what you can do without.

2. **Read up on it.** Men's magazines are helpful, as are the usual *Cosmo*s and *Marie Claire*s. Google how to do the perfect fellatio. Research painful penis no-nos. It's all useful and will make you feel more comfortable when it's time to, er, grab it with both hands.

3. **Make the most of your menstrual cycle.** Sure, shagging can relieve period pain, but it's best mid-cycle, when your body is telling you to get pregnant. It's nature, so just make sure you're using birth control if you don't want a baby, and then enjoy the hormones.

4. **Set the scene.** If it makes you feel sexier, light candles and play your favourite slutty tunes. Dress for him – and yourself! I don't personally believe in all these aphrodisiac things (I've eaten a dozen oysters, washed down with the finest champagne, and not felt a tingle), but if a few drinks make you less inhibited, enjoy them. However, remember, getting plastered is never a good idea, so if you're going to have a drink, don't go overboard.

5. **Foreplay is key.** Spend enough time on this and you're rocking. Tell him what you want, and tell him what he really can't do. Stray hands – or penises – can spoil the whole evening. Guide his hands, speak up, and encourage him by moaning and grinding when he's doing something good. And learn to enjoy his body too. A lot of women think men's bodies are ugly and weird. They're not. They're hot. Train yourself by staring at photos of David Beckham, Bear Grylls and Daniel Craig. And, of course, the best route to amazing sex is by doing it only with someone you really, really fancy. Whether it's a

friend you've suddenly fallen for, or a man you've just met who makes your knees buckle – just make sure you want him so badly you can't wait to feel flesh on flesh. Sex isn't like the movies. It's not clean and polished and perfect. But it's hot. Bring on the heat.

## Kinky sex

Do you really want to go there? New sexual crazes/perversions are being introduced into the bedding arena every day. What can you say no to without being a prude? Anything! Most women's favourite thing is the missionary position. Most men's favourite thing is doggy-style. Do that, and a bit of oral, and no one can accuse you of being dull. Anal is getting more and more popular, but if it's not for you, don't go there. Back-alley business can be tricky and dangerous, so why risk it if you won't even get a kick out of it.

Many modern practices would make the Marquis de Sade blush, so don't feel boring for saying a firm, 'Thanks, but no thanks.' Wolf-bagging is coming up a lot lately (look it up, it's too long and bizarre for this book), as is bottom-hole kissing and golden showers. Then, there are always the old classics: dressing up as a nurse/French maid/school-girl, and so on, or a bit of slap and tickle with handcuffs and a whip.

What do you fancy? Share it with a partner you trust, and enjoy your body – it's for pleasure, so don't be scared to use it. But don't delve into any new hobbies when you're off your head on booze – you really will regret that in the morning!

> **NB On the whole, things to avoid** – and in fact to dump any man for – include night-time shenanigans that include anyone under 18, anyone over 80, animals, internal injuries, passing out, or hating yourself. Foodstuffs? Go girl!

## Bad sex

We all have off days – or nights, I should say. Sometimes it really isn't him, it's you, and other times it's simply that your mojo doesn't work together. It's all about your chemistry between the sheets, and however good you are at dinner/drinks/tennis, if it's not clicking when you're copping off, you have to sort it out. The worst thing you can do is ignore it. You'll both be aware if, after a good few turns around the duvet, neither of you has come or even come close. Lots of women feel that they don't deserve good sex – especially after a divorce that they still feel guilty about, or after having children (and therefore having nether regions they don't consider to be in tip-top condition). Bad sex has somehow become their destiny. Wrong, wrong, wrong. All modern girls deserve to feel sexy, wanted and like little horn dogs when the moment is right.

So, when you start dating someone and it's not clicking, you have two choices:

1. Dump him. He can take his sorry excuse for a willy somewhere else. You can start again.

2. Work through it. After a few attempts that are clearly leaving both of you cringing into the pillow, whisper something along the lines of, 'What's going on?' Boost his ego (remember, men are totally sensitive) by saying 'I

fancy you so much, you're gorgeous, I just don't get it'. Even blame yourself a bit to be kind and humble (just don't start believing it! It's not your fault; sex is a joint venture). With luck, he'll be relieved you brought it up and you can have an honest, adult discussion about it. Decide together what to do: whether it be taking it slower, sharing particular things you love, guiding each other to hot spots, even taking baths together and talking, or giving each other massages. Just keep communicating.

If he won't listen to you or open up, you should go back to the first choice: dump him and his sorry excuse for a dick. If, after a while of being honest, open and experimental, the sex is still a disaster zone, you two have to decide how important sex is to you. I've got friends who really can't be arsed to do it at all. Once a month, or a bit more frequently when they've been trying to conceive, has been all they've needed.

It's important as you get older to find a partner with the same sexual appetite as you. This isn't always easy, of course, and you can't help who you fall in love with but ... I'm not saying you should chuck a caring, witty, charming, loving man because he only wants to do it when you throw on a feather boa and beg him to. But seriously, from my personal experience, I've learned the hard way that if one of you wants it a lot, and the other one doesn't, resentment and frustration are going to creep into other aspects of your relationship too. At least, if you get into a serious relationship with a man who's on a different body-clock time zone to you, be upfront about your needs and demands. Then at least if you have to do a runner for someone who lets you get a good night's sleep every now and again, or who does you when you need it, he can't say he wasn't warned.

## Shagging on the job

There are too many horror stories about office copulation to believe that anyone is really doing it there any more. Yes, it's an old fantasy. Shagging on a desk, with the threat of the cleaner walking in or a security camera picking up on your passions. The reality, however, is always a little bit more tense and scary – and when the wild affair is over, photocopies of your bottom seem to mysteriously land in the post room.

If you're carrying on with a colleague, try to keep your cool in the workplace. If you must do it, head to a cupboard that you are sure no one goes to any more, after hours, and lock the door.

If you're carrying on with the boss, and he wants to do it on a pile of contracts in his glass office, well it's your choice. I mean it's a very sexy idea (if your boss is sexy, of course, not a sweaty middle-aged man with a paunch), but protect yourself. You don't want to be gossiped about or, even worse, sacked, when he's had his fill of you.

## How to turn a one-nighter into an all-lifer?

We live in a modern, equal world, right? Well, luckily most men seem to think so, but there are still a few dinosaurs with double standards out there who think that if you shag on a first night you must be a complete slut who is doing this with any Tom, Dick or Harry who asks (and, be honest, are you?)

Cool down. If you really like someone and you feel the relationship has potential, take it easy. You have all the time in the world to show him what a little minx you are when the lights go out.

◆ If you need some instant gratification, go for oral – and make it so amazing that he will be begging to see you again, and soon! Be enthusiastic, and open about what you'd like to be doing – but you're too good a girl to be doing it straight away.

◆ Enjoy the teasing; enjoy the build up. You can't get those first moments of 'will we, won't we, should we' back again. The first kiss can be enough for a while, can't it? Enjoy the electricity that you used to feel as a teenager.

◆ If you have a mishap and end up shagging, don't go psycho and cry and wail that you regret what you've done or, worse, blame him for seducing you. You're a grown-up girl, you did what you felt like at the time. Try to make your wantonness into something desirable long-term. Men love a big-up. Try a few sweet lines that get across you're really quite a virginal nun-like figure, but he's so sexy he destroyed your cast-iron will, 'I never have one-night stands. I haven't slept with anyone for months, but you, I needed you so badly. This is just going to get better and better.'

## Secrets of success

◆ Enjoy your body. It's the greatest instrument you will ever have. It's amazing, so look after it.

◆ Sex burns so many calories, it's fun and a workout – what's not to love? It also tones bits of you that you didn't even know needed toning.

◆ Remember compliments; forget insults. You are not as fat or flabby as you think you are.

◆ Threesomes rarely seem a good idea, because someone will always feel left out. And it could be you. I'm a jealous person, so threesomes are certainly not made for me — neither are they for more insecure/envious or worried women, I imagine.

◆ So many women I know are scared off doggy-style for fear of what their white, wobbly bottom will look like in its full-moon glory. Good news girls: that position actually pulls in those muscles in such a way that I can guarantee your ass will have never looked finer. Enjoy!

◆ We can programme ourselves to want more or less sex. Seriously, the more you have it, the more you need it — and then when you're single you can go for months being celibate and not even notice. Use this training when you find a partner to try to get in sync with each other.

◆ You haven't always got a headache. Go on, when he's begging for it and he's been a good boy, give in. Sex is like going to the gym. It seems like a chore before you get going, but then you never regret going there when you've finished.

◆ Who says what is normal and what is not? Do what feels right for you, and doesn't hurt other people, and have fun. Don't let what you do between the sheets ever make you feel bad or cheap. It's got nothing to do with anyone else — except perhaps the person you're doing it with, if he's lucky!

# Chapter Eight

# Feeling fabulous

EFORE YOU CAN FIND your dream man, you should be in a dream state. No, I don't mean spending time staring idly out of the window, fantasising about what you're going to call your children and how many chickens you're going to rear on your country estate. I'm talking about getting fit and feeling fab. The more physically in control you feel, the more in control you'll feel in every aspect of your life.

## Being healthy

Couch potato, are you? Always too busy working or playing to make it to the gym? Excuses, excuses. The truth is that the more energy you use, the more energy you get. Yes, it's a battle when it's raining outside, and you've got an early start, and there's a pizza delivery man you quite fancy who can deliver a margarita deep crust in time for *The Office* re-run. I'm not suggesting you transform yourself into some kind of Paula Radcliffe marathon-runner-type person – and, God forbid, you develop a six-pack – but there are a few simple tricks you can do to look and feel better instantly.

It's not just about dropping a dress size and rediscovering your cheekbones, it's about increased energy, improving your immune system and feeling more confident in your own skin.

## Getting in shape

The good thing about being single is that your time is your own time. Use the time you've suddenly got free to get fit. Even 30 minutes a day will have immediate and long-term benefits. And remember, the fitter you are, the more you'll get out of your love life. Sex becomes much more enjoyable when you're not sweating and panting for the wrong reasons!

## Short cuts and simple tricks

Get fit the easy way with these ideas:

◆ **Take the stairs.** Always. Every time you go to step in a lift imagine that it's just for old people.

◆ **Get walking.** Get off your train or bus one stop early. Get your iPod on and get to know a new album while marching. And don't let the weather put you off. There's something so right about walking in the rain with Justin Timberland crooning in your ears.

◆ **Stretch.** Do yoga while watching television. Learn a few basic moves and work your muscles (holding the postures for as long as you can) during your favourite soap opera. Even a few minutes in bed before you get up can be good too – and it doesn't feel difficult because you're still in your jimjams.

◆ **Dance.** Put on some dance tracks while you're cleaning your apartment, and have a disco. This has double benefits: you'll have a sparkling home, and your exaggerated cleaning-cum-dancing will tone those arms and abs too.

◆ **Get yourself a gym buddy.** Find someone to make you go to a class after work even when you'd rather go to the pub.

◆ **Even better, get yourself a sexy trainer** who you want to look hot for – and impress with the amount of sit-ups you can do.

◆ **Join a gym** that is so expensive you will guilt-trip yourself into getting the most out of it.

◆ **Join a gym with a spa attached.** After every workout, treat yourself to 30 minutes in the Jacuzzi and steam room. Your muscles and skin will reap the benefits too.

◆ **Find something you love.** If you hate the gym, you won't keep motivated. Try a few different sports to see what excites you the most – and don't worry if you just like the sport because you like the hot guys or after-game social-ising. Whatever gets you through the game, is fine.

◆ **Take inspiration from the stars.** Get dancing or ice skat-ing (not eating insects in the outback).

◆ **Go to a gym with televisions,** and tie in your workouts to favourite shows. You'll feel so worthy knowing that instead of sitting on your behind, you're working it on the treadmill.

◆ **Read health and fitness magazines** and read the real-life success stories. Not only are they great for inspiration, but you'll also come away with a few tips on how women with real lives and time constraints can fit exercise into their already packed days. Ignore these silly celebs who say that they eat what they want and never get to the gym, yet stay skinny. They're lying.

◆ **Check yourself out in the mirror** – and on the scales if you fancy. (Although I prefer to rely on how my clothes feel on me, because muscle – which I promise you will be building – weighs more than fat.) Flex your arms and feel proud of the development and change in shape.

**ALISON,** 39

❝ I met a very ripped, fit guy on match.com. I was probably at my chubbiest when I met him and his perfect torso inspired me to shape up. He never made me feel unattractive but I couldn't join in all the activities he wanted me to – well, not without hyperventilating and collapsing, anyway. After we'd been dating for a few months, we decided to book a romantic skiing trip. This was the push I needed. I had three months to reduce my thighs and build my stamina. Although he said he loved me either way, he really enjoyed the confidence boost getting slimmer and fitter gave me. We're still together. And I'm still shaping up. ❞

## What type of get-fit girl are you?

No matter what type of girl you are you can get fit now.

◆ **No-time girl.** Start running. Buy yourself good trainers and grab 20 minutes before or after work whenever you can. You'll notice the difference and you're not constrained by class times or other people.

◆ **Stressed-out girl.** Try Pilates for stretching out those stretched muscles, or go swimming. Swimming twenty-five laps three times a week will provide you with time away from the world. It's the one place you really can't take your mobile phone or iPod. Enjoy the peace and quiet and spend your splash time thinking about your day, or the week ahead, and getting everything ordered.

◆ **Easily bored girl.** Join a team, and let the thrill of winning and the depression of losing spark you into caring and keeping up with the others. Netball, hockey, football – find a sport and a group of girls you care about.

◆ **Party girl.** Start frequenting a bar with a mechanical bull (those things are great for your thighs). Or go dancing. You can burn some calories while you're burning it up on the dance floor.

◆ **Routine girl.** If you like to follow a set pattern week to week, get a timetable from your local gym and write certain classes into your diary. Treat these appointments as seriously and immovable as you would a business meeting or a dinner with friends.

◆ **Lazy-bones girl.** Get a trainer. If your alarm clock can't get you out of bed an hour early on a cold, January morning, perhaps the thought of someone waiting for you will. Having a personal trainer is an indulgence – and it can be expensive. But perhaps just get one to kick-start your new health routine. Very soon, you'll be addicted to the feelings of worthiness and wonderfulness and will be able to motivate yourself.

---

**NB Busy modern girls tend to travel a lot for work and pleasure.** The first thing that goes out of the window when you're out of your normal routine is exercise. Don't beat yourself up too much – even if you're on holiday and overdoing the paella and sangria. Try to go for an exciting exercise class, start riding a bike to work, or swim. These are actually fun things to do, so shouldn't be too hard. If your hotel has a gym, use it, if you feel like it, but everyone needs a few days off, so work extra hard in the run-up to your trip, and promise yourself you'll make it up when you get back.

# Dieting dilemmas

Sadly, being fit and fab isn't just about burning up calories; it can be about eating fewer too. So put those HobNobs back in the biscuit barrel and stop feeling sorry for yourself. No extreme dieting, please – it doesn't work! And neither does taking laxatives! And we all know that starving or purging has long-term issues too. The best thing to remember is balance – and to listen to what your body needs: good food.

The old trick of sticking a 'fat photo' on the fridge really does work. Or eat in your bikini, with love handles out and on display (if you're at home, of course – it won't go down too well in Pizza Express). This trick really helped me shift a few pounds before my holiday last year.

◆ **Treat yourself.** The minute you put a ban on anything, it becomes even more desirable. Have a 'treat day' when you can eat what you want, or even allow yourself a daily moment of bliss. If you're a chocoholic, still enjoy your time with Mr Cadbury's – just reduce your time with other naughty things like booze and crisps.

◆ **Reprogamme your brain.** When you're full, stop eating. Forget what granny used to say about clearing your plate. Eat slowly, enjoying every mouthful, Fill up first by drinking water, eating fruit or having a warming bowl of vegetable broth.

◆ **Don't be fooled by 'low fat' or 'healthy' labels** on packaged foods. They may have reduced the fat or sugar, but it's still in there. It doesn't mean you can have double.

◆ **Don't skip breakfast.** It's the oldest trick in the book, but it's true: starting with a good meal in the morning will stop your blood sugar going crazy later on.

◆ **Sometimes you're not hungry, you're thirsty.** Drink 2 litres (3½ pints) of water per day.

◆ **If you're extra busy** or travelling, keep healthy snacks with you – nuts, fruit and chopped-up vegetables are great.

◆ **Think of food as fuel and goodness.** Very soon you'll feel smug eating a healthy meal of beans, peas or lentils, fruits and veg, and you'll feel a little bit disappointed with yourself when you've gorged yourself on nothing but hamburgers and chips all weekend. Visualise the vitamins and minerals flooding into your system, improving your skin, hair, nails – and chances of a long life! So much of healthy eating is about our attitude to food, and educating ourselves on what is really good and what is really bad.

◆ **At any meal,** aim for half your plate to be filled with the green, good stuff. In fact, try and eat the colours of the rainbow. Everything in moderation.

**FREDDIE,** 31

❝ When I became single again I had spare time on my hands – and a driving need to escape. So I booked into a health spa with my mum. I really paid attention to the specially prepared menus, and actually enjoyed trying new foods and drinks. After a week there, I learned that I actually preferred peppermint tea to my normal cuppa, and just that one simple change was saving me a hundred calories a day. I bought the cookbook on my last day and have really felt a sense of empowerment taking control of my eating habits. I feel like I'm actually eating more – but of the right stuff. Without a man force-feeding me kebabs, I got into a groove of enjoying soups and salads, and yogurts with nuts and honey – meals my loser ex would have called girly. ❞

## Controlling your demons

There's a time and place for everything – including bad habits. Just make sure you are controlling your demons – not the other way round.

A common problem when you're back on the single scene is to want to go out drinking every night. I had a solid ten days of margarita guzzling last year, and although it was fun at the time – my complexion and waistline didn't enjoy it so much.

So drink, of course, but do peruse the cocktail calorie list to see what you can drink without doing too much harm. This is how I found out that margaritas are practically the worst thing you can drink, except chocolate milkshakes! So I switched to white wine – which is much lighter on the calories. Vodka and gin with low-calorie mixers are a good option. But beware: the more you drink, the more likely you are to roll home tipsy and consume a packet of frozen fish fingers before passing out. Dead calories. And I used to think that hangover-day calories didn't count – but they do. If drinking too much makes you overly reliant on greasy fry-ups the next day, cut down.

---

**NB Remember, totally boozed-up, drunken chicks** aren't that visually enticing to the opposite sex. Sure, let your hair down with your girls, but if you're on the pull, calm it a down a bit.

---

## How dating damages your looks

Dating can sometimes leave your appearance less than perfect:

◆ **Stubble rash.** I recently had this so badly that I managed (I hope) to convince my office I'd come down with a terrible stress rash. It was disgusting, like something out of a Hollywood horror makeup studio. What can you do? Ask him to shave. Kiss less. Moisturise immediately. Wipe with tea tree oil to stop it getting infected. And leave it alone – no picking or playing.

◆ **Love bites.** No, no, no! You're not 15 years old any more. If you sense he's going there or feel a tug on your flesh, remove yourself from his Dracula-like fangs immediately and tell him to stop it.

◆ **Brazilian injuries.** I'm not talking about strained muscles from too much caipoeira! I'm talking about ingrown hairs – or even worse, burns – from trying to get a perfect shaven haven. Go to a good place, moisturise your down-below area and ask your beauty therapist for advice on products that keep the skin smooth and rash-free. Something containing salicylic acid normally does the trick. And tweeze any obvious problem areas, but don't gorge yourself into oblivion. If you're prone to spots and problems down there, try a hair-removing cream – these tend to be gentler, if not so long-lasting.

◆ **Dark circles.** Suddenly you've gone from being a lonely girl in with a telly, to a dating vixen, shagging rather than getting her eight hours. Try to balance it out. As tempting as it is to tie yourself to his bedpost every night of the week, have a night-on-night-off rota. Otherwise your work, grumpiness levels and face will suffer. In case of emergencies, slices of cool cucumber or used camomile tea bags do work at reducing puffiness, and some new wonder creams have been clinically proven to reduce circles.

◆ **Hair knots.** That bedhead look is kinda sexy, but not when your hair starts breaking because of too much love action. If your hair is being ruined by endless nights of passion there are two things to do. Short term: start carrying a comb in your handbag to get rid of those tell-tale knots and rats' tails at the back of your head. Long term: get yourself a good conditioner, lady, or even consider shagging with a jaunty pony tail!

# Secrets of success

◆ Feeling good is about what's going on inside and out. Learn to love yourself, body, mind and soul. Spend time and money on yourself. Too often in relationships, we invest more in our partners than ourselves. And they are too often unworthy of our interest and devotion. Send that care straight back to yourself.

◆ If you have serious issues about your weight and fitness, go to the doctor. They've seen and heard it all, so there's no need to be embarrassed.

◆ Keep yourself motivated by treating yourself to fancy, sexy gym clothes. You'll look forward to getting ready to get fit.

◆ Every time you inch nearer to your dream weight, reward yourself – even if it's just with a small chocolate bar.

◆ While you're getting into perfect shape, make the journey easier by improving other areas of your appearance. Ask your hairdresser what colour and style would suit your complexion and face shape. Take advantage of freebie makeovers and personal shoppers in department stores. Get yourself colour-confident by going to an expert who can tell you what shades suit you.

◆ Buy some magic knickers. They hold everything in gloriously.

◆ High heels instantly lengthen your legs and also lift your posterior.

◆ Wearing one shade will make you look slimmer.

◆ Get to know your body shape and dress appropriately.

◆ Do not, I repeat, do not, get sucked into thinking skinny is best. Most men like something to grab hold of, and there's a lot to be said for women who love eating and drinking and being carefree – they love life. That's attractive. Don't become a slave to the scales. Just get to a point where you feel and look fabulous – and stay there!

# Chapter Nine

# Managing your emotions

S INGLE OR SCORNED WOMEN can often get labelled by nasty men, smug married women or women who have no clue how tough it can be out there, as crazy, cat-loving, desperados. Life is tough enough; we don't need any more unfair criticism or misunderstandings. Because, the truth is we *do* have moments of craziness, cat loving and desperation. The single girls' world is a tough one. But what doesn't kill you makes you stronger.

## Relishing your freedom

Instead of wishing away your time alone, learn to embrace it. I can honestly say I have never been as purely happy as I have been in this past year, being on my own. I have had time to get myself healthy, confident and refreshed again before seriously thinking about the next stage in life and love. For me, being single has been like pressing the stop button for a while. I have been living in the moment, with no one to answer to but myself. When you're in a relationship, there's too much talk of where you're spending Christmas, whether you are going to buy a house together, whether you are getting married, will you be having kids, and so on – it's all about laying down foundations and looking ahead.

Being single, and being free, however, has meant taking it day by day, and not having to fill my diary with dull chores that were really more about him (whoever 'he' was) and what he wanted.

If you're single, chill out about it – you won't be single forever, unless you choose to be. I have absolute faith in that for me and for you (and I'm writing this as a single girl at the moment).

Enjoy your lack of constraints. Don't let the panic of

being left on the shelf ruin your fun and frivolous days. Take it day by day. If you want to keep busy, see people and plan all your holidays for the next year, go ahead and do it. But, by all means, if you feel like languishing and lazing around just because you can, do that too! Living for the moment – and never knowing who or what is going to happen next – isn't just about freedom, it's about excitement too.

---

**NB If you're ever in doubt about the true freedom being single affords you,** talk to your married mates. They can't go out straight from work and dance till dawn on a whim. Neither can they book a week in Mexico on their own when they're feeling the need for some sun, sand and sea. There are good and bad points to being loved-up, and being single, so see both sides. Don't think you're missing out in your single moments. Remember, there is nothing worse than being lonely in a relationship.

---

## Not ready yet?

Don't throw yourself back on the scene when your heart, or ego, is bruised and battered. You'll be no good to anyone, least of all a dashing young man who deserves you. If you're not ready yet, be an enabler. Still go out with your friends and have fun, but don't desperately search for someone. Enable your friend to meet others by being her wingman. Not only will you pick up tips on the current dating scene (and get out of your pyjamas), but also your mate will return the favour when you need it.

## Stop overthinking

Why do us girls tend to analyse ourselves into oblivion? We can't stop it, can we, paranoid little monkeys that we are. Just remember:

◆ **Is he doing the same?** Probably not. You know how we can weigh up for minutes whether to add a kiss to the end of a text message or not? Well, I've asked my men friends about this (I've often read a lot into an 'X' at the end of a message, incorrectly), and they say it's just an impulse, it doesn't mean anything, and they think we're mad for even noticing it.

◆ **Worrying achieves nothing.** Absolutely zero. So we fret and fuss but it won't actually change how he feels or what he'll do next. Don't become a nervous wreck if you can help it – men don't find it attractive. Girls seem to think that being stressed makes us slim, burning off fat with all that nervous energy. It's not true. The opposite is true. It makes your body panic and store calories. Chill out, for God's sake, woman! Nail biting, hair pulling and finger fiddling are not good looks.

◆ **If you choose to overthink things, overthink to yourself** (or just a few close friends). Don't overthink to the world. I have developed a huge crush on a gorgeous guy and have bored half my colleagues into joining me on a 'does he, doesn't he' trail of highs and lows depending on his phone calls or emails. Even I can hear that I've become annoying. Keep it real and keep it to a closed group. Mums always love hearing your over-analytical thoughts, especially about men (they're hoping for grandchildren soon, remember?) and they are good listeners – but they do tend to remember everything and use it against you at a later date. Beware!

◆ **Are you friends or friends friends?** If you really can't tell if you're just friends with a guy or more than that, get drunk and get honest. It can drive you to distraction, so rather than second-guessing and thinking about taking it further, grab the, er, bull by the horns and ask him. Be coy, and say, 'I've developed a bit of a crush on you – tell me now if you don't feel it too and I can stop it and start fancying the boy from accounts again, hee hee.' Keep it light and he'll know you're not about to turn into a stalker!

◆ **If you're constantly thinking 'this is wrong'**, sadly, it probably is. Get over him.

---

**JENNY,** 29

❝ I kept hearing warning bells. I kept saying to my friends that something was up, and that Tom had changed, that I didn't feel he looked at me the same way anymore. I over-thought everything too much, and disappeared into my own little world of self-doubt and worry. After a few months of this agony, my warning bells were proved right. My husband of five years was having an affair. The ironic thing was that one of his many justifications for the affair was the fact that I had become so quiet and stressed. Arsehole. ❞

---

## Stop blaming yourself!

Now modern girl, I don't know where this has come from – perhaps your parents, perhaps your first teacher at school – but not everything is your fault. Some relationships work, some don't. It's half-luck, half-hard work – and the responsibility lands at the feet of the two people involved. So how can being single again be just your fault? There were two people in the relationship, so it took two people to get out of it.

Been single too long? You'd like to blame that on the fact you're too fat/old/boring/moany/successful/busy (insert your own personal paranoia here), wouldn't you? Well, sorry, if you really think you're to blame for something, do three things, then shut up:

1. Apologise.

2. Change.

3. Move on.

## Being you – and learning to love yourself

It's true that a certain self-confidence comes with age. I really do like myself more in my thirties than I did in my twenties, and when everything is heading south and I'm starting to get wrinkles, at least I have this emotional plus out of getting older.

Certain things have really made me know who I am and to trust my instincts.

Surround yourself with good people: those who truly love you. You know who your real friends are: they are the ones who are there for you when life gets awkward, or if there's a difficult thing to say, they say it.

## Get rid of the bad people

When you're young, friends seem to be all about quantity not quality. As you get older, start to sift out the negative forces. If you can count only five people as true friends, who cares? Five good ones are worth far more than 20 party pals who don't call when you're lonely on a Sunday with nothing to do.

Love your family, and get to know them – but if you're stuck in a negative cycle from your childhood days of being scared of your dad's opinion, or your sister's successes, remove yourself for a bit. Don't get on top of each other. Have a breather, and when you do return to the nest, state clearly that you're an adult and that some of the things they do has to change because it upsets you.

## Forget feeling jealous

Some wise person once said envy gets you nowhere – that life is a race, sometimes you're winning, sometimes you're losing, but the important thing to remember is that the race is only with yourself. Don't beat yourself up because someone has a better boyfriend or car than you. Just work at improving yourself. I've always been a believer in getting ahead by being brilliant, not getting ahead by putting other people down.

## BE TRUE TO YOURSELF

- Never take credit for someone else's success and never lie to yourself. You'll sleep well at night – even if it is on your own.

- Don't put on a show for anyone, because when the curtain falls and you take off the makeup, you can feel pretty shallow if you've been acting. Be who you are all the time. Some people will love you, and some people won't. But it will be their loss.

## ROSE, 32

❝ After initial negative emotions – self-loathing, misery, depression, the full gamut – I've emerged from my divorce with an onwards-and-upwards attitude! My friends built me up again – and believe me, there was nothing to work with. I was a greasy, upset mess who refused to leave the house. They made me laugh, paid me compliments, bought me little beautifying gifts like new clothes and makeup – and even my boss has been brilliant. Persuading me to go on new courses and giving me a pay rise has worked wonders for my confidence. ❞

## Eating your emotions into shape

Food isn't just there to enjoy, and it isn't just avoided to get thin. What you consume can really affect how you feel each day – and help you to beat negative energy. Being single can play havoc with your diet and waistline. It can go up and down with your mood swings, but here are a few rules:

If you're feeling depressed and grumpy:

◆ **Eat** eggs and bananas. They are full of good proteins that your body converts into good-mood boosters like serotonin.

◆ **Avoid** sugary sweets. They may be a tasty treat and may boost your energy in the short term, but you'll soon slump. And slump means grump. They also encourage hunger, so you'll eat too many, which is bad for the belly.

If you're single and stressed:

◆ **Eat** chocolate and salmon: chocolates don't just taste good with a cup of tea, but they contain a chemical called epicatechin, which improves blood flow to the brain – and therefore the very useful skills of having a good memory and concentration level. This will help you get everything in perspective. Meanwhile, oily fish are swimming in good fatty acids that boost brainpower, energy levels and beat depression.

If you're feeling spotty and unlovable:

◆ **Eat** grapes, kiwi fruit, peas and apricots for high doses of antioxidants and vitamin C. They'll help banish acne, dry skin and that dull complexion, and you'll soon be feeling sexy again.

◆ **Avoid** junk food. It might taste good in the short term, but really … you know it's bad for you and your face.

If you're lonely and angry with PMT:

◆ **Eat** anything with vitamin B6 in it: bananas and chicken are great for that time of the month.

◆ **Avoid** tea with or close to meals. Yes, a cuppa would be nice, but it stops your body from absorbing much-needed iron at this delicate time of the month. No iron, no energy – or healthy hair.

If you're hung-over after a bad first date:

◆ **Eat** eggs, they'll help your liver to clear out toxins.

◆ **Avoid** chewing gum. You may feel it's useful in disguising your alco-cigarette breath, but it will just make you gassy and bloated from swallowing air and artificial sweeteners.

## Do you have a chip on your shoulder?

If you want to move forward, you need to move on – and I mean emotionally. Stop the negative patterns and situations that you tend to get yourself into. Don't keep going for the same type of guy, or reacting in the same way. Force yourself to spice things up a bit and to look at stuff from his perspective, or from the perspective of a mutual bystander. We all have our issues and our Achilles heel. Recognise it and try to stop it getting in the way of a totally good life as a free single girl, or as a girl about to fall in love – don't be a slave to your chips!

> **NB And don't put up with some dude's issues either.** If he has a chip on his shoulder, sure, give him a chance to get over it (remember, his ex-girlfriend could have really exposed and damaged him in a way that you can't even imagine). Try to help him through it by getting him to appreciate that you're different, or why he's wrong about women generally. But if he doesn't change, you'll have to decide if you can handle it. Sadly, some chips on shoulders stay around forever.

## Secrets of success

◆ Don't be scared of life, or of challenging yourself. In fact, do something that scares you every day – even if it's something silly like trying a new sandwich with a strange ingredient. If you live by this motto, a whole new world – and emotional strength – will open up to you. As I'm typing this, I'm sitting with a stiff neck from riding a mechanical bull at a party last night. It was scary, but I was the first one up. Life is too short to be held back by fear or doubt.

◆ You've fallen for an emotional guy? Good for you – he should understand why you weep at bad Hollywood films then. But make sure his sensitivity doesn't quickly become a drain. Sometimes men who sell themselves as 'emotional' are really just attention-seeking moaners.

◆ Indulge your bad emotions every once in a while. Cry until you can't cry anymore. Scream until you hurt your own ears. It's better out than in.

◆ If you feel that talking to someone who doesn't know you would be helpful, then do it. There is nothing embarrassing or weak about going to a therapist. More people do it than you might imagine.

◆ When you're feeling low, speak up. Your friends and family won't know how to help if you shut them out or put up a wall. People, in general, will want to help you.

◆ This too shall pass. Remember that. All things good and bad will rise and fall. Don't berate yourself. And don't overcongratulate yourself either. At all times, do to others what you would like to be done to you, and you can't go far wrong.

◆ Try to laugh at least three times a day.

# Chapter Ten

# Facing the future

Looking forward can be scary. There's no doubt that we all like security and safety. Why else would women spend a fortune each year going to tarot card readers and psychics? We all want to know that everything will be OK. But, you know what? If you're happy with yourself, you will be OK – whether you're single for a while or not.

## Spinster forever?

I hate even using the word 'spinster', but that is the official term for the unmarried woman, I suppose. It brings up thoughts of strange, quirky ladies in slippers with cat calendars and a penchant for *Antiques Roadshow*. I prefer to use the term MGF: a modern girl with freedom. Freedom to choose what she does with her time, and who she's going to choose to spend her valuable time with in a committed relationship.

I do believe that however much fun being single can be for a while – decades even – most people ultimately want to be someone else's number one. They want to find a partner who's good enough for them, perhaps get married, perhaps have children … so don't feel like a weak fool for wanting to settle down. We all want to be loved.

When will you stop being single? I suggest that will come when you've had time to recover from whatever heartache has gone before, and when you've spent time with yourself – working out what you need, what you have to change and how you want to live your life.

You won't be single forever if you don't want to be. You may have to go out of your way to find love: to go for a different type of guy, to search on the Web, to open your heart and take risks, but you will find someone who will love you. Everyone does. Even the meanest, strangest, chubbiest, skinniest and naughtiest humans find someone who is equally mean, strange, chubby, skinny or naughty to settle down with.

Your time will come, so don't waste your freedom waiting for it. Enjoy yourself, and get the stuff done now that you won't have time to do when you're in a committed relationship: write that book, run that marathon, travel the world for a year ...

## It's not always a ticking clock ...

... that drives you to settle down. So put people in their place if they just assume you're hooking up with someone because you need a baby daddy. Time is a big factor to many, of course, but sometimes the desire to settle down is because you're fed up with partying, you've realised you like being in a relationship and nurturing someone or it's as simple as not wanting to be alone anymore. Whatever it is, don't let anyone put their value system on to you – especially people who've always been in settled, committed relationships and don't know what it's like to make your way out in the world on your own. If you decide the time is right now to make a push at finding a life partner, just do it. And don't pay attention to naysayers on either side of the fence: the singletons who want you to remain in their club for ever, or the smug marrieds who didn't have to be so open about their desperation to find a mate.

> **ALLI,** 39
>
> 6 I loved being single because it meant I could travel the world and really concentrate on my career for the whole of my twenties and early thirties. But suddenly it hit me at 35: bugger, I've been having a bit too much fun on my own but I want a baby and a home and a nice man to share it with. Like magic, out of the blue, appeared David. At 35 you don't hang around and we were married and pregnant within a year. He didn't work out and we're now divorced, but Charlie has just turned three and having him is the best thing I ever did! 9

## Not settling for second best

Even in your loneliest moments, when your biological clock is tick-tocking away so loudly your head is going to explode, should you ever undersell yourself. I'm not talking about being vain and thinking that on the looks front you score a 10 so why should you go for an 8? I'm talking about not settling for a man who is verbally or physically abusive, who is mentally cruel, who steals and lies, or reduces you to a shadow of your former self. You deserve better than that. The key reasons women settle are understandable:

1. They want a baby now!

2. They're scared no one else will want them.

3. They have been convinced by the man that they are lucky to have him.

Well, for starters, I was raised by a single mum and she did a very good job. You don't need to settle for a horrid man just because you want a baby. I know (and my friends and I discuss this all the time, and they agree with me) that if I get to 38 and I'm still single, I'll have a child on my own. Whether at this stage that means adopting or using some other means (borrowing one of my lovely gay boys' sperm and my mum's turkey baster), I won't let the lack of good men get in the way of my ultimate dream: to be an amazing mum. I know from personal experience that a woman can raise children alone, and they grow up fine.

Points 2 and 3 really come from women's lack of self-confidence, which has normally occurred after bad boy-friends have whittled them down to nothing over years of negative comments and criticism. But you have to believe in yourself, ladies. Of course, people will want you. And if you really believe you're not loveable at the moment, don't moan and mope – do something about it: start that diet, get some style advice, take up some interesting hobbies that give you something to talk about, change your job for something that gives you a life outside the office.

As for you being lucky to have him. Well, I bet you make more effort with his friends and family than he does with yours. And I bet you pay more attention to your appearance and personal hygiene. I also suspect you're always thinking about 'we' and how you can make life better for your 'team' while he's thinking about what's best for him. I think he sounds like the lucky one.

The truth is you're both lucky to have each other – for as long as the relationship is good. The minute it stops being good, sit up and pay attention, then try to sort it out. Don't just settle through fear.

> **NB Band-aid babies are not a good idea.** You both know it's not working, you know you're settling – or he feels he is – but you feel that bringing a new life into the world will re-invigorate your feelings for each other. It can do, I suppose. But, more often than not, babies just bring sleepless nights, great expense and a lot of worry and stress. And a baby is for life, not just for relationship counselling. So think before you have a child with someone you know is not right for you – unless of course you're just using him as a sperm donor!

## The children dilemma

Sadly, us ladies got the raw deal here. Men can go on being international playboys, sowing their wild oats, well into their fifties even before they have to settle down and pro-create. Us ladies start to feel nervous – in general – once we hit 30.

There are a few important things you can do to protect your fertility:

◆ Avoid stress as much as possible.

◆ Don't smoke.

◆ Don't drink more than six units of alcohol per week.

◆ Don't eat too much – but certainly don't eat too little.

◆ Get regularly tested for sexually transmitted diseases.

And the big new thing is to take fertility tests – some are even available at chemists. Ask your doctor, if you are worried. I did a test when I hit 32 after I became single again. Luckily, the test proved I was still ovulating normally – and it was a real weight off my mind. However, I still know time isn't on my side, so it is a matter I think about often.

## Setting yourself targets

Ask yourself the following questions to set a rough game plan for the next ten years. This will help not just with a significant relationship, but also with forming your opinions about yourself, what you need and what you need to get rid of:

1. Do I enjoy my career?

2. Do I like where I live?

3. Do I want children (or more children)?

4. Do I want to get married before I have children?

5. What have I learned from past failed relationships?

6. What have I learned to change about myself?

7. What makes me happy?

8. What do I appreciate most in other people?

9. Where do I want to be this time next year?

10. What are my 'new me, new year' resolutions?

11. If I could fast-forward ten years, where would I be – and with what type of man?

We can't plan for everything in life, but we can wake up and acknowledge what we want and don't want. That's why, even in a relationship, it's good to ask yourself these questions. You don't have to rest on your laurels. Resting often means not grabbing life with both hands.

## Getting to know a new man

Some things will have him running for the hills:

1. Asking for marriage and kids too soon.

2. Saying, 'I love you' too soon.

3. Showing erratic, bi-polar behaviour: extremes of sweet then sour.

4. Being overly affectionate and needy.

5. Shagging lots of other people at the same time – and bragging about it!

Obviously, there are lots of other deal breakers too, but in my experience these have all been big ones – and women everywhere commit them all the time. Really, when you see them written down, you can see why the men wouldn't like it, can't you?

## When can the games stop?

Ultimately, after the initial thrill has died down, you want to get off the emotional roller coaster and enjoy a secure, happy relationship – with no games. Sure, bring on the surprises and the fighting-followed-by-great-make-up sex, but you can keep the tricks and insecurity.

Once you've made a commitment to be in an adult relationship, stop playing. If he insists on continuing with the games, sit him down and teach him the rules. He has to play fair. You're giving him your heart to hold, so he has to be careful not to break it.

If he continues with the BS (bullshit), kick him to the kerb before your heart gets dropped and trampled on. This means anything as small as not calling when he says he will, to paying more attention to other women than to you when you're out together, which feels huge.

Life's too short for games – unless they're fun for both sides.

---

**JENNA,** 31

❝ I never knew where I was with my ex-boyfriend. He'd cancel dates without telling me, and I'd show up in bars and sit on my own like an idiot, waiting for him for half an hour. I spent so much of that year stressed out, waiting for him – and giving him all the power! Would he call, wouldn't he? Did his friends like me? Was I too stupid for him? I realised he was being mean so that I would dump him, which I did. And now I'm with a guy who loves to take me out, thinks I'm smart and always tells me that his friends and family love me. There's no drama, just a mutual appreciation society. Hoorah for me! ❞

---

## Warning bells

Listen to that ringing in your ears, girlfriend! A little tinkle is fine; a crashing tubular bell is crushing. You do get a feeling if someone is up to no good or has a dark side. You either choose to go for it anyway, or to go with your gut and pull back on the reins a little bit and take off the rose-tinted glasses. Believe me, you'll pay for it later! I did!

## The greatest gift of all: true love

I cannot wait to meet someone who looks at me 'that way', who eats me with his eyes and makes me feel adored and cared for, even when I'm grumpy, mean and a bit spotty. And I don't doubt I'll find him. My mum and step-dad had both been married before, both got their hearts broken, and then found each other in their late thirties and have looked after each other ever since – being each other's best friend and love interest. That's what I want, and I know it can happen. I still walk in on them kissing and cuddling (or my dad being forced to tickle my mum's feet – her 'watching television treat') and rather than finding it embarrassing I think it's adorable – and they're both 60 years old!

To get things in life, you have to put yourself out there. You have to take risks and give people second chances – just don't be too willing to give them a third and a fourth.

If you love yourself, love will find you. If you can be honest and open, it will be reciprocated. These are the dreams of every single girl in any city (or town, or village) everywhere. And dreams do come true.

Long live the single girl, and long live her future romance – whenever and however she finds it.

# Secrets of Success

◆ Have you started talking to yourself at home? That's OK – if it's only a little bit! If you start full-on chit-chat and debates, get out more.

◆ Don't feel that a man won't like you just because he's too handsome. It's horses for courses, and even the best-looking men I know are lacking in self-esteem and would love a charming, kind woman to be honest about her feelings with them. Men sometimes feel as if they have to do all the work. Help them out with a little forefront honesty every now and again.

◆ If you're happy in yourself and with yourself, happiness will find you. You must know who you are before you can truly let anyone else know you. Put yourself first and love yourself. You'll get there. Strong, fabulous, kind, clever, modern girls always do!

# Further reading

Beck, Martha, *Finding Your Own North Star: How to Claim the Life You Were Meant to Live,* Piatkus Books, 2003

Beck, Martha, *The Joy Diet: 10 Steps to a Happier Life,* Piatkus Books, 2004

Minnini, Darlene, *The Emotional Toolkit: How to Cope With What Life Throws at You,* Piatkus Books, 2006

Naik, Anita, *The Lazy Girl's Guide to Success,* Piatkus Books, 2007

Ray, James Arthur, *Harmonic Weath,* Sphere, 2008

Whelehan, Imelda, The Feminist Bestseller: *From Sex and the Single Girl to Sex and the City,* Palgrave Macmillan, 2005

# Index